NINE
BLACK
AMERICAN
DOCTORS

ROBERT C. HAYDEN
AND
JACQUELINE HARRIS

▲ ADDISON-WESLEY

Also by Robert C. Hayden
SEVEN BLACK AMERICAN SCIENTISTS
EIGHT BLACK AMERICAN INVENTORS

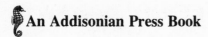An Addisonian Press Book

Text Copyright © 1976 by Robert C. Hayden and Jacqueline Harris
Illustrations Copyright © 1976 by Addison-Wesley
All Rights Reserved
Addison-Wesley Publishing Company, Inc.
Reading, Massachusetts 01867
Printed in the United States of America
BCDEFGHIJ-WZ-79

Library of Congress Cataloging in Publication Data

Hayden, Robert C
  Nine Black American doctors.

  "An Addisonian Press book."
  Includes index.
  SUMMARY: Biographical sketches of nine Afro-Americans
who have made significant contributions to medicine.
  1. Afro-Americans in medicine—Biography—Juvenile
literature. [1. Afro-Americans in medicine—Biography.
2. Physicians. 3. Afro-Americans—Biography]
I. Harris, Jacqueline L., joint author. II. Title.
R153.H39   610'.92'2   [B] [920]   76-15172
ISBN 0-201-02842-5

TABLE OF CONTENTS

*This book is dedicated to all young people
who aspire to careers in medicine.*

This book could not have been written without the help of relatives, friends and associates of the nine doctors. And most important were the interviews and resource materials provided by the doctors themselves. There were institutions, too, that were helpful in providing vital resource materials. We sincerely thank the following people and institutions for their interest and sharing of memories and information:

Dr. and Mrs. Eugene Adams, Dr. Farrow Allen, Mr. Charles Alston, Dr. George Cannon, Dr. Kenneth Clark, Dr. William Montague Cobb, Mr. Charles Collins, Dr. and Mrs. Daniel Collins, Miss Louise Crowd, Dr. Leon Cruise, Dr. Angella Ferguson, Mrs. Harriet Fuller, Mr. Solomon C. Fuller, Jr., the late Mr. Thomas W. Fuller, Dr. Kenneth Girard, Miss Frances Grant, Dr. Joseph Henry, Dr. Jane Hinton, Mr. Charles Jones, Mrs. Marian Logan, Dr. Myra Logan, Dr. Thomas W. Patrick, Jr., Dr. Charles Pinderhughes, the late Judge Francis Ellis Rivers, Judge G. Bruce Robinson, Miss Genevieve Stuart, Dr. William Walker, Dr. Jane Wright, Mrs. Louis T. Wright.

Institutions: Atlanta Public Library, The Francis A. Countway Library of Medicine, Hartford Public Library, Howard University Medical Library, *The Interpreter* published by United Methodist Church, *Journal of the National Medical Association,* New York Academy of Medicine, Office of Informational Services of Boston University Medical Center, University of Connecticut Medical Center Library. A special thanks to Evelyn and Mary Noonan and Deborah Hayden for their youthful editorial input, to Delores Noonan for typing services, to Aileen and Stephen Davis for research advice and help, to Dr. Willis N. Cummings for information on the Badger brothers, and to William H. Hayden for providing a home away from home on research trips to New York.

Robert C. Hayden
Jacqueline Harris

THE FORERUNNERS

Onesimus was a black slave who contributed to progress in medicine during America's colonial period. His knowledge led to the use of inoculation in the Boston (Massachusetts) area as a way to prevent people from catching smallpox.

In 1721 Onesimus was the slave of Cotton Mather. When Mather asked his slave Onesimus if he had ever had smallpox, he answered, "Yes and no." What did Onesimus mean by, "Yes and no?"

Onesimus described an operation that he had undergone in Africa. On his arm was a scar where he had been cut with a sharp knife. A bit of pus from the sore of a person who had a bad smallpox infection had been placed in the cut. The pus contained the smallpox germ, and once in Onesimus's body, the pus had given him a very mild case of smallpox. This practice was used because it produced a mild case on purpose and made the body immune to a severe attack of smallpox in the future.

Mather thought that the African method should be tried in America. He contacted ten doctors in Boston and told them about this African practice of deliberately infecting healthy persons with smallpox to keep them from catching the disease accidently. One of the doctors, Dr. Boylston, tried the inoculation on his own son and two of his slaves. It worked. Later Dr. Boylston inoculated 241 people, and only six later caught smallpox.

Some religious leaders opposed the practice of inoculation. They charged that it was a non-Christian or heathen practice.

Mobs attacked the homes of Mather and Boylston. Despite strong opposition some doctors continued using the method described by Onesimus. When some people died after a smallpox inoculation, many became fearful of the technique. Some doctors claimed deaths from inoculations were as great as from the disease itself.

In the 1790's the British doctor, Edward Jenner, perfected an inoculation technique which used a less dangerous kind of smallpox germ. Today the smallpox vaccination has totally conquered the spread of this dreaded disease.

However, during the American Revolutionary War inoculation against smallpox was used to prevent soldiers from getting the disease. Because Onesimus passed the idea on to Dr. Boylston the ravages of smallpox were lessened.

This is just one example of the contributions of black Americans to medical science. Black Americans have been demonstrating their interest and ability in the field of medicine for a long time. As early as 1667 an African, Lucas Santomée Peters, was trained in medicine in Holland. He practiced in the colony of New York under the Dutch and the British. When the British took over New York, the governor gave him land in return for medical services.

Slaves in early New England often served as apprentices to their masters who were doctors. In time some became doctors on their own. One of them, Primus, a slave in Connecticut, helped his owner in surgery and in the general practice of medicine. When the doctor died, Primus took over his master's practice. He was reported as being "extraordinarily successful throughout the county." His master's white patients did not mind being treated by him.

Papan was a Virginia slave who also learned medicine from his master. Papan's treatment of skin and venereal disease was extremely effective. His work in medicine was so outstanding that the Virginia Legislature bought him from his master in 1729 and set him free from slavery to practice medicine for the benefit of the people of Virginia. In 1733 another Virginia slave, who had discovered cures for scurvy and distemper, was freed by the state and given a pension for life.

Many African slaves brought to America proven methods of relieving pain and treating diseases. The control of disease using the roots of plants and various herbs was widely practiced on the African continent long before the discovery of America. In Africa the medical value of minerals and plant substances had been learned through practical experience. When Africans found themselves in America it was only natural that they would continue using their well proven methods of treatment.

Many slaves gained such wide reputations for their healing powers within the slave community that they attracted the attention of whites.

As early as 1792 a slave named Cesar had gained a reputation for his use of roots and herbs to cure poisoning. His remedy for rattlesnake bite was published in *The Massachusetts Magazine*. The state of North Carolina purchased his freedom and gave him a pension of $500 a year for life.

The first black American to be widely recognized as a doctor was James Derham. Born in 1762 in Philadelphia, he was a slave to Dr. John Kearsley, Jr., one of the most noted doctors of his time. Though slaves were not supposed to be taught to read or write, the family who owned him gave him instruction. Derham took an early interest in the medical profession of his master. When Derham was a teenager, Dr. Kearsley allowed him to mix medicines and give them to patients. After Dr. Kearsley's death Derham was sold to a Dr. West, a surgeon in the British army during the Revolutionary War. During the war he served Dr. West in some of the menial duties of caring for injured soldiers. At the end of the war, Derham was sold by Dr. West to Dr. Robert Dove of New Orleans who used him as an assistant.

After several years, Dr. Dove gave his assistant his freedom in recognition of the outstanding work he had done. Derham was able to practice his knowledge and skills in medicine on his own and earned as much as $3,000 a year—a very handsome income at that time. In 1788, at 26 years of age, James Derham was regarded as one of the most eminent doctors in New Orleans.

The most noted black American doctor after James Derham was a Dr. James McCune Smith. A graduate of the University of Glasgow in Scotland, he began to practice medicine in New York about 1837. Quickly he distinguished himself as a skilled physician and surgeon and served on the staffs of hospitals with a number of white doctors. Dr. Smith lived during the time when science was being used to try to prove the inferiority of black people. He attacked this argument with a strong speech in New York on "The Comparative Anatomy of the Races." In the chapter on Dr. Montague Cobb, you will read about another doctor who fought the same myth of the inferiority of black people through his research and writing on human anatomy nearly one hundred years later.

The next black American doctor of prominence was Martin R. Delany. Born in 1812 in Charleston, West Virginia, Delany was a free black who grew up in Pennsylvania. He began to study medicine as a 19-year-old apprentice in Pittsburgh. He abandoned medicine for a while to fight the Fugitive Slave Law of 1850, to work on anti-slavery causes and to help freed slaves who wished to return to Africa. He returned to Pittsburgh in 1851 to continue his medical studies under Doctors Joseph P. Gazzen and Francis J. Lemoyne. After being refused admission to the University of Pennsylvania and medical schools in New York because he was a black man, he was finally admitted to the Medical School of Harvard University.

Upon leaving Harvard, Dr. Delany, like Dr. Smith before him, became involved in the argument over the superiority and inferiority of the races. He traveled throughout the country using his medical knowledge to defend the intelligence and ability of black Americans.

Dr. Delany returned to Pittsburgh to practice. He was a leader in treating cholera during the epidemic of 1854. His worth to the community was shown when he was appointed to a city board that gave medical advice to poor people, black and white. During the Civil War Dr. Delany served in the infantry as a major in the United States Army.

Like many black doctors, Delany devoted most of his free time to improving conditions for his people. When not practicing medicine, he was traveling in America, Africa and England speaking out against slavery. In Ohio he was beaten, almost fatally, by a mob of whites when he spoke for the freedom of slaves.

In 1890 Dr. Daniel Hale Williams was a young black doctor on Chicago's South Side. Although he had a large practice, he was not satisfied. Young black women who wanted to become nurses could not gain admission to any nursing schools in Chicago. Additionally, the young black doctors who were graduating each year from medical school were unable to gain internships in hospitals because of their race. Internships were becoming necessary for a license to practice medicine. Finally, Dr. Williams had to operate on his patients in their kitchens or dining rooms, but one of his patients needed an operation that just couldn't be done in her home. She needed the facilities of a well-equipped hospital; but no hospital was open to her. As long as Dr. Williams wasn't accepted on the staff of a white hospital, these problems would remain.

Dr. Williams was committed to progress for black people in every phase of medicine—public health, daily medical services, the training of nurses and doctors, and the availability of the best possible surgery. The solution to his deilmma was a simple one; he would open his own hospital. In May 1891 The Provident Hospital and Training School Association opened its doors. There would be no more operations performed in a dining room or kitchen for Dr. Williams.

Two years later Dr. Williams leaned over the chest of a man rushed to his Provident Hospital during the evening of July 9, 1893. The victim, James Cornish, had been stabbed near the heart during a street fight. Dr. William's eyes were fixed on the knife wound in Cornish's chest. The knife had left a cut about an inch long just to the left of the breastbone.

At the hospital the wound had nearly stopped bleeding and Dr. Williams thought that it would heal easily with rest and proper treatment. But during the night Cornish's condition took a turn for the worse. Severe pains developed in his heart area. His pulse weakened. Signs of shock appeared. By early morning there was evidence of internal bleeding. His pulse could scarcely be felt in his wrist. Heart pains and sharp coughs persisted. He was near collapse from a sleepless night.

Dr. Williams decided to operate. He would open up the left side of the dying man's chest cavity to explore the heart region. In the 1890's a chest operation anywhere near the heart was unheard of. But Dr. Williams dared to risk his reputation so his patient might be saved.

Dr. Williams cut through the tissue, muscle and cartilage around the heart. The pericardium, a thin protective sac which surrounds the heart, had received the stroke of the knife blade when Cornish was stabbed. Since the sac tissue lies directly on top of the heart muscle, the muscle, too, had been pierced by the point of the knife blade, but the heart wound was superficial and needed no stitches.

The protective sac around the heart was another matter. The cut in the pericardium would have to be sewed up. Dr. Williams flooded the heart area with salt solution to guard against infection. Then, gently grasping the sac tissue with his surgical forceps, he closed the cut with catgut. He was then ready to close up the chest opening with silkworm gut. A dry dressing was placed over the outside incision.

Fifty-one days after he had been stabbed, James Cornish was released from Provident Hospital. Two years later, Dr. Williams saw his heart patient hard at work in a Chicago stockyard, and James Cornish continued to live a normal life for 20 more years.

Dr. Daniel Hale Williams was the first man ever to operate successfully on the human heart.

One of the first accounts of dentistry among black Americans appeared in *The Pennsylvania Gazette* in 1740. Simon was a black man who was able to "bleed and draw teeth" and "was a great doctor among his people." Another was Doctor Zeke who practiced dentistry in Savannah and Augusta, Georgia, where he gave his services to whites in the daytime and to blacks at night.

Robert and Roderick Badger were pioneer Georgia dentists in the 1800's. Robert Badger was born in 1829, his brother Roderick in 1834, in DeKalb County, Georgia. They were sons of a white dentist and a black woman who was one of his slaves. The Badger brothers learned dentistry from their master-father.

Both the Badger brothers faced great prejudice from whites as they tried to practice their profession. Robert Badger was an itinerant rural dentist who earned his living traveling on horseback from county to county around Atlanta, Georgia. Roderick Badger arrived in Atlanta, Georgia, in 1856 to start a practice. There was much opposition to a black man practicing dentistry at that time.

In May 1859 a petition was presented to the Atlanta City Council in opposition to Roderick Badger. Part of it read *"We feel aggrieved, as Southern citizens, that your honorable body tolerates a Negro dentist (Roderick Badger) in our midst, and in justice to ourselves and the community, it ought to be abated. We, the residents of Atlanta, appeal to you for justice."*

Despite opposition, the Badger brothers continued with their profession. Both became leading citizens of Atlanta.

The first black American to receive a dental education and dental degree from an American medical school was Robert Tanner Freeman. Born in 1847 to slave parents in North

Carolina, he was among the first six graduates in dental medicine from Harvard University in 1867. After graduating from Harvard, Freeman practiced dentistry for many years in Washington, D.C.

Another early graduate of the Harvard Dental School was George F. Grant. He finished Harvard Dental School in 1870 and was the school's first black instructor, serving for many years as a Demonstrator of Mechanical Dentistry and as an instructor in the treatment of a condition known as cleft palate. His invention of a device to correct cleft palate brought him national recognition. He also operated a large and successful practice in Boston which consisted mostly of white patients. He was known for his skill in making and fitting false teeth.

These sketches of some 18th and 19th century doctors only begin to tell the story. To show the depth and richness of the lives and contributions of black Americans to medicine, nine doctors are described in the following chapters.

All the doctors in this book are 20th century Americans. Five of them are still living. Each has lived a unique and meaningful life. Each has been more than just a doctor—more than a fighter of disease in a laboratory or hospital, more than a healer of human illness, more than a medical teacher. Each has had to face and conquer a "disease" left over from the days of the American slavery of black people—the disease of prejudice and discrimination against those of African ancestry.

Each doctor has met race discrimination in a different way. And each has done something to raise the health standards of the country through medical practice, research or teaching.

What has it meant to be both a doctor of medicine and a black American at the same time?

SOLOMON CARTER FULLER

1872–1953

Psychiatrist & Pathologist

John Lewis Fuller was a slave in Petersburg, Virginia, during the late 1700's. He was a skilled boot and shoemaker for his white master. With some of the money that his master allowed him to keep, he was able to buy his freedom. He was also able to buy his wife's freedom from slavery.

By the late 1700's quite a few African slaves in the United States had bought their freedom by paying their masters a sum of money. Others had gained freedom from slavery because they had fought in the American Revolutionary War.

These free black people—educated, highly skilled in crafts and business, and fairly prosperous—were dissatisfied with their lowly place in American life. Because they were outspoken against slavery and for the civil rights for Afro-Americans, slave and free, they were seen as a source of trouble for slave owners. There was great discussion in white America about "what to do with these free and discontented blacks." One answer was to return the former slaves to Africa.

Some black Americans organized themselves and raised money to send ex-slaves back to Africa where they or their parents had been born. Some whites founded the American Colonization Society to set up a colony of emigrant blacks in Africa. The West African Republic of Liberia was officially established in 1816. The United States House of Representatives created the American Society for Colonizing Free People of Color. It was argued in the nation's capital that "the sons of Africa" should, in justice, be returned to "the land of their fathers."

In 1822 a settlement at the site of Monrovia, the capital city of Liberia, was the beginning of a new life for a few thousand former slaves. John Lewis Fuller was one of the former slaves who left America under the American Colonization Society during the early 1800's.

About sixty years later, during the summer of 1889, a boat left the shores of Liberia's west coast headed for America. One of its passengers was the grandson of John Lewis Fuller. Solomon C. Fuller was 17 years old as he left his homeland forever, headed for the southern United States where his grandfather had been a slave. He was traveling to America to further his education, and he went on to become a pioneering medical doctor in the diagnosis and treatment of mental illness (psychiatry) and diseases of the nervous system (neuropathology).

Between 1899 and 1933, the year of his retirement, Dr. Fuller gained national and international respect and recognition for his research, teaching, diagnosis and treatment of mental illness. His portrait hangs in the offices of the American Psychiatric Association in Washington, D.C., along with those of other great figures in American psychiatry.

Solomon Carter Fuller was born in Monrovia, Liberia, in 1872. His father, also named Solomon Carter Fuller, was a coffee planter and Liberian government official in Monrovia. His mother, Anna Ursala James, was the daughter of Mr. and Mrs. Benjamin Van Ranseler James, both doctors and church missionaries from America. Solomon and his brother Thomas were educated at a school their parents established on the coffee plantation.

In September, 1889, Solomon Fuller arrived in Salisbury, North Carolina, to attend Livingston College. Livingston was a college for black students in the South, and Fuller was the only student in his class from Africa.

By 1893 he had achieved his first goal—graduation from college with his bachelor's degree. From Livingston he moved north to begin medical studies at Long Island College Hospital in Brooklyn, New York. He spent only a year there and moved to Boston, Massachusetts, to continue his medical courses at the Boston University School of Medicine. A second goal was accomplished in 1897 when he was awarded his M.D. degree and could be called "Doctor Fuller."

Dr. Fuller was pleased with his college opportunities and achievement in America. At the same time he was also disillusioned by the racial discrimination that he and other black people faced. His African background had been extremely religious—shaped by his mother's church work—and he was so deeply shocked and disturbed by the alienation between the races that he didn't attend or participate in church religious affairs in this country. "All during my teen years I tried to get Dad to come back to the church," said his son, Solomon C. Fuller, Jr., "but I didn't succeed."

Though bitter about the disrespect given to black Americans, Dr. Fuller kept busy with his medical practice, research and further study—hoping to help bring a change in white America's racial views through his work in medicine. He chose not to leave America and return to Liberia but to remain and try to create a better life for himself and his fellow man.

Upon his graduation from medical school, Dr. Fuller received an internship at Westborough State Hospital for the Insane in Massachusetts. Here he began his career in the research of brain diseases. And here, too, he met his future wife, Meta Vaux Warrick, who became one of America's most noted artists.

At Westborough Dr. Fuller began to examine cells and tissues from the brains of people who had suffered from mental illness. He looked for changes in the brain matter that might explain certain types of abnormal human behavior and deaths caused by nerve diseases. In his laboratory there was a machine that could slice brain tissue into segments thinner than tissue paper—so thin that light could pass through the slices. Since light could pass through these thin sections, he was able to take pictures or photomicrographs of the brain cells.

Dr. Fuller was known for his work on different forms of mental illness (psychoses) and a rare brain disease known as Alzheimer's Disease. A person suffering from a psychosis may lose thinking and reasoning powers and may exhibit behavior dangerous to that person or other people. Dr. Fuller sought to find a relationship between patients' thinking and behavior and the photomicrographs of their brain tissue.

The work that Dr. Fuller carried out at Westborough on degenerative diseases of the brain was widely recognized by other psychiatrists early in his career. In 1909 he was invited to participate in a landmark meeting at Clark College in Worcester, Massachusetts. The meeting marked Sigmund Freud's visit to the United States, and a photo taken at the meeting shows Dr. Fuller with Freud, Carl Jung and Alfred Adler, the leading figures in the development of modern psychiatry.

Dr. Fuller lived at the Westborough State Hospital during his early years there. He was totally immersed in his work and worked long hours each day. His only relaxation from research and working with the mentally ill was fishing in a pond at the back of the hospital.

In 1911 he reported the ninth known case of Alzheimer's Disease (named for the doctor who first observed this condition in humans). This disease occurs during middle age and results in memory loss, impaired thinking and physical aging. Dr. Fuller suggested that something other than hardening of the arteries was the cause of this disease. Over 40 years later, in 1953—the year of Dr. Fuller's death—two other medical researchers confirmed Dr. Fuller's findings.

Meta Vaux Warrick, an artist from Philadelphia, met Dr. Fuller while paying a visit to Westborough State Hospital. She had been studying art, particularly sculpture in Philadelphia and Paris. When she learned about Dr. Fuller's knowledge of medical photography, she suggested that he might enjoy portrait photography. This began a lifelong hobby, and Dr. Fuller became a skilled experimenter in photographing old portrait prints.

When Dr. Fuller and Meta Warrick were married in 1909, they moved into a new home at 31 Warren Road in Framingham, Massachusetts, not far from his laboratory at Westborough State. Here Fuller opened an office for private practice, worked at his photography, engaged in bookbinding and gardening, and raised his three sons.

His work at Westborough continued long after his internship. In 1899, just two years after arriving at Westborough, he was appointed the hospital's head pathologist. Dr. Fuller took over the growth, staffing and running of the lab, and began a 45-year career at Westborough—22 years as a pathologist and 23 as a consultant in diseases of the nervous system. In 1913 he became the editor of the *Westborough State Hospital Papers*, a journal reporting the medical research work of the doctors on the hospital's staff. His own medical writings appeared in this journal, as well as in medical textbooks and other journals around the country.

In 1899, the same year he was named head pathologist at Westborough, Dr. Fuller received his first appointment to teach at the Boston University School of Medicine—from which he had graduated only two years earlier. Between 1899 and 1933, when he retired from Boston University, he was an instructor and lecturer in the structure and diseases of the nervous system. As an authority in the field of mental disorders, he gave to Boston University more than 30 years of devoted teaching and research.

The fact that Dr. Fuller was a black man presented a dilemma for him. He was proud of his African ancestry and proud to be a black American. But he was disturbed to find himself thought of as "an excellent colored doctor." This bitterness he kept to himself. When news reporters came to his home in Framingham, he would turn them away. He didn't want to become known as "a colored psychiatrist." He felt that his medical achievements should become known on their merit alone.

Although he was a popular and highly respected teacher and researcher, as well as a recognized authority in psychiatry, Dr. Fuller's race held him back. He was never officially on the payroll at Boston University Medical School although he did draw a small salary for his teaching there. During his last five years at Boston University he served as head of the Department of Neurology but was never given the title to go with the responsibilities. Eventually a white assistant professor was made a full professor—a title that Dr. Fuller was never given—and was appointed Head of the Department of Neurology. When this happened, Dr. Fuller retired saying, "I thoroughly dislike publicity of that sort and despise sympathy. I regard life as a battle in which we win or lose. As far as I am concerned, to be vanquished, if not ingloriously, is not so bad after all." But he added, "With the sort of work that I have done, I might have gone farther and reached a higher plane had it not been for my color."

In his later years Dr. Fuller became somewhat resentful at not receiving the titles to go with the teaching positions he held. His resentment was provoked mostly by friends and associates who felt that he was treated unfairly because of his race. At one time he was receiving $24 a month while others received $28 for doing the same job. But he took pride in his work and accepted less with a gracefulness that was uniquely his—for Dr. Fuller could find many things in life for stimulation, pleasure and learning.

Dr. Fuller's typical day was long and full. It started around 9:30 in the morning and often didn't end until long after midnight. The mornings were spent at the Westborough Hospital lab while afternoons were devoted to teaching in Boston at the medical school. But his day did not end with his teaching. When he arrived home in Framingham in the late afternoon, there would be patients waiting to see him, and they would sometimes come as late as nine or ten o'clock in the evening. His day wasn't over at ten, either, when the last patient left— for there was still reading to be done, both for pleasure and for his medical work.

Dr. Fuller was an avid reader, often reading until two o'clock in the morning. He was a great collector of books, and there weren't many that he couldn't read in one sitting. Book-binding was another of his hobbies, along with photography. "He seemed to spend everything he had on books," recalls his son Solomon, Jr. He was fond of picking up rare old volumes in dilapidated condition from secondhand book stores in Boston and converting them into beautifully bound collectors' items. He learned all phases of the bookbinding craft and tooled and decorated his own leather for covering old books. He bought old prints too, and these he photographed and gave to his friends.

Reading, research and teaching were only a few of the ways in which Dr. Fuller contributed to his field. He also traveled. As a young psychiatrist he went wherever there was some-thing to be learned, or where there was someone doing re-search that would give him new knowledge or some person who could give him some new ideas. He traveled and studied in Europe and at medical institutions in this country. Some of his advanced studies were done at the Carnegie Laboratory in New York.

In 1904 he went to Germany to study at the Psychiatric Clinic of the University of Munich, as well as at the Patholog-ical Institute of the same university. In Europe he studied with medical researchers who were developing a new approach to medicine—those who were studying the biochemical or physi-cal causes of disease. One of those under whom he studied in Germany was Dr. Alzheimer.

One of the most exciting moments in Dr. Fuller's life oc-curred one afternoon on a sightseeing visit in Berlin, Ger-many. He walked by the house of Nobel Prize winner Paul Ehrlich, and on an impulse, he knocked on Ehrlich's front

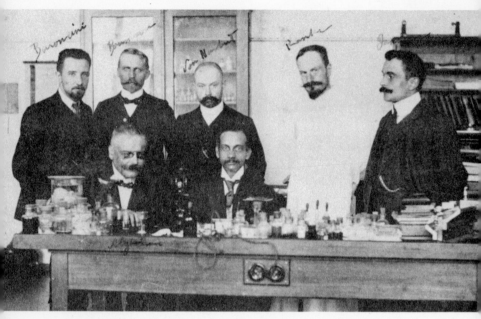

Dr. Solomon C. Fuller (seated right)
visiting in Europe with leading
psychiatrists of his time. Dr. Alzheimer
is seated beside him.

door just to say "hello." Ehrlich had received the Prize in 1908 for his work in immunology and was a man Dr. Fuller had long admired for his research. But Fuller was a complete stranger to the famous Ehrlich. To his surprise Dr. Fuller found that Ehrlich lived alone and was lonely for someone to talk with. Dr. Fuller ended up spending the entire afternoon with his idol, and this chance meeting led to a lifelong friendship. Dr. Fuller later told his sons and others that the afternoon with Ehrlich was one of the most profitable events and lasting memories of his life. He had not been content just to stand on that Berlin street in 1905. He had reached out to meet a person he had long admired and had found an experience that helped and enriched the rest of his life.

Before returning from Europe, Dr. Fuller made his only trip back to Liberia to visit his mother and brother. He resumed work in the United States with new ideas and skills acquired in Europe.

He began to look at mental illness in a different way. His work centered on physical disease and changes in the body (organic changes) that caused different forms of mental disorder. His focus on the organic causes of mental disorder led him into research on schizophrenia (multiple personality), mental disorders connected with old age, disorders connected with continuing alcoholism and inherited brain diseases.

Dr. Fuller was also interested in behavioral or mental problems which appeared to have no organic causes. Some people suffered from mental illness because of maladjustment to daily living. He began to explore life experiences and their effects on thinking and behavior. He began to study and practice the effects of psychotherapy on mental disorders. (Psychotherapy treats a patient's problems through counseling and discussion—helping the patient to analyze his or her own behavior and feelings.)

His studies in Europe helped Dr. Fuller to build two bridges in the early 1900's. He learned that there was more to mental illness than just understanding the changes and deterioration of brain cells. He began to make the shift from neuropsychiatry to psychotherapy. A neuropsychiatrist looks for and studies changes in the structure and chemicals of nerve cells in the brain—changes that might cause differences in a person's behavior. A psychotherapist looks for and treats abnormal behavior that appears not to be caused by any physical change in nerve cells or tissue.

The second bridge was his help in bringing the center of psychiatric research and knowledge from Europe to the United States. He was a leading pioneer in the study, diagnoses and treatment of brain disease and human behavioral problems. His writings in medical books and journals, and his work as a member of the American Psychiatric Association, the Boston Society for Psychiatry and Neurology, the New York Psychiatric Association, and also the Massachusetts Medical Society, the New England Medical Society and the American Medical Association, influenced the thinking and practice of all doctors in the field of mental health.

The encouragement of other black doctors was another of Dr. Fuller's strong interests and contributions. In 1923 he trained four black medical school graduates in neuropsychiatry. They went on to serve at the Tuskegee Veterans Administration Hospital in Tuskegee, Alabama, a hospital serving hundreds of black people in the South. Those whom Dr. Fuller guided went on to prominent careers in medicine. Dr. George Branch became Chief of Psychiatric Service of the Veterans Administration Hospital at Tuskegee. Dr. Charles Pinderhughes of Boston became a Professor of Psychiatry at Boston University and Coordinator of Residency Training at the Bedford (Massachusetts) Veterans Administration Hospital.

"Though growing old Dr. Fuller still acted like an eager young medical student as he talked with me about the newest ideas and methods of treating mental illness,'' recalled Dr. Pinderhughes. "Talking with Dr. Fuller was a great education for me because he had worked and studied with the great minds in 20th century psychiatry and psychoanalysis. In an era when the professional development of black people was discouraged and inadequately rewarded, Dr. Fuller persevered until he secured the finest training available. And what he knew helped me.''

Dr. Fuller's private psychiatric practice was a large one. All kinds of people came to him for counseling treatment—the rich and poor, black and white, prominent doctors and criminals. He worked with the Framingham Police Department, examining criminals who exhibited dangerous behavior and appearing in court to report on a criminal's mental health.

Patients often traveled long distances to be with Dr. Fuller for psychotherapy. He always took plenty of time with each patient—sometimes spending over an hour with each one while others waited an hour or more before seeing him.

"My father had great spiritual qualities,'' remarked his son, Solomon, Jr. "People came to him for a spiritual communion that was a refreshing, inspiring and motivating experience. Some people kept coming back to him right up until the time of his death, not for treatment of a mental disorder, but just to have a spiritual exchange with him. My father had such a gracious, loving, radiant and quieting personality that it had a great calming effect on his patients' problems.

One of the doctors who often visited Dr. Fuller was Dr. William Hinton, the subject of another chapter in this book. Dr. Fuller counseled his friend privately and on holidays. Dr. Hinton, his wife and two daughters and Dr. Fuller, his wife and three sons would take turns visiting each others homes. The two doctors would talk about their work, their students and the special problems they faced each day. But that was not all they talked about for they had a hobby in common, and that was gardening.

Dr. Fuller, like Dr. Hinton, was a master gardener and lover of plants. They were always comparing their gardens, and there was a certain rivalry between them as to who had the greatest variety of plants, the most healthy and beautiful. Dr. Fuller knew the Latin names of all his plants, and he took great pride in transplanting and cultivating his favorites.

While Dr. Fuller worked in his garden, his wife worked in her art studio. Throughout her married life Mrs. Fuller pursued sculpturing and achieved recognition as one of America's outstanding black artists. Her sculpture can be found at Howard University in Washington, D.C., the New York Public Library, the YMCA in Atlanta, Georgia, and at various art museums throughout the country. A bronze bust of Dr. Fuller done by his wife stands in the lobby of the Solomon Carter Fuller Mental Health Center in Boston.

Dr. Fuller retired from Boston University in 1933. The last 20 years of his life were somewhat tragic.

In the mid-1930's Dr. Fuller's diabetes worsened, and he became thin and frail. In 1944 he began to lose his eyesight, but he was not willing to give up his practice and continued to treat patients until the time of his death. Dr. Pinderhughes traveled to Framingham to help Dr. Fuller continue his practice when he could no longer see. "I would give the patient his physical examination, and Dr. Fuller, blind and aged, would do the rest," recalls Dr. Pinderhughes.

Without sight, Dr. Fuller would kneel in his backyard garden, tending his plants and planting new seedlings. He could not see the weeds though, so they grew freely and finally overran his garden.

Blindness robbed Dr. Fuller of his favorite pleasure—reading. He had to be content with having his sons and friends read to him. At Christmas, two years before his death, he gave his son Tom a book on fishing. *The Complete Angler or The Contemplative Man's Recreation Being a Discourse of Rivers, Fish Ponds, Fish and Fishing,* written in 1887, was one of the first books that Dr. Fuller had rebound and covered with leather before his son Tom was born.

The radio was also used to take the place of books that he could no longer read. And he was much more open to questioning and would sit for long periods of time talking about the past. Pulling his long, pointed white beard, he recalled stories from his early life in Liberia and the great people he had met through his work in medicine, such as Freud and William E. B. Dubois, the black political leader, author and historian.

Dr. Fuller lived a full and useful life to the end. A doctor friend, Dr. James B. Ayer, who visited Dr. Fuller in 1953, shortly before his death, wrote:

"I saw him and talked with him; though blind, his memory was excellent, his speech flawless, his interest alive. He knew he had not long to live, but accepted the fact in his unusual philosophical manner, like the perfect gentleman he was."

WILLIAM A. HINTON

1883–1959

Pioneer Against Syphilis

William "Gus" Hinton was awarded his Doctor of Medicine degree in 1912 from Harvard Medical School, but he couldn't treat a sick person in a Boston, Massachusetts, hospital. At the time of Hinton's graduation, black doctors were not allowed to practice in any of Boston's hospitals. It wasn't until 1931 that the first black doctor was admitted to an internship at Boston City Hospital.

As a young medical school graduate, William Hinton had wanted to be a surgeon. He later wrote "My ambition . . . was to prepare myself to practice and teach surgery in the South, particularly among an underprivileged group which was in need of medical services. But this ambition wasn't realized."

Hinton was unable to get an internship in a Boston hospital because of his race. The reason given was that married men were not admitted as interns, but he was not discouraged from pursuing a career in medicine. He turned instead to laboratory work, and he excelled.

Fifteen years after graduating from medical school, Dr. Hinton had developed an important blood test for the dreaded disease of syphilis. The Hinton Test, as it became widely known, was used throughout the country for the next 25 years. In 1935 Hinton's test was adopted as the official laboratory test for syphilis at the Massachusetts Department of Public Health, and at all hospitals in the state. Few people knew that it had been developed by a black man. In 1936 his book, *Syphilis and Its Treatment,* was the first medical textbook written by a black American to be published.

Syphilis is a social disease. It is caused by a germ that can be passed from one person to another through close body contact. Once in the blood stream, the syphilis germs multiply and begin to attack the nerve cells. This disease can affect boys and girls, men and women, people of all ages, races and classes.

Although syphilis is not as widespread as it was 50 years ago, it is still one of the most dangerous and crippling diseases known to man. It can cause sterility, blindness, insanity and death. Teenagers and young adults are particularly susceptible to syphilis.

Dr. Hinton devoted his professional life, over 30 years, to fighting syphilis. He was respected throughout the country as an authority in the field of social diseases. When he retired as Director of the Department of Clinical Laboratories at the Boston Dispensary in 1952, Christian Herter, then Governor of Massachusetts, wrote in a letter of tribute, "Your name is known the world over for singular achievements which have benefited all of mankind."

Hinton was born in Chicago, Illinois, in 1883. His parents, Maria and Augustus Hinton, who had been slaves in North Carolina, had moved to Chicago after being freed at the end of the Civil War. Shortly after the birth of their son, the Hintons moved to Kansas City, Kansas, where Dr. Hinton grew up. His parents were determined to give him the advantages of an education they had not enjoyed. While attending Kansas City schools and a private Catholic school, he earned money as a newsboy, raised chickens and did odd jobs to help his family.

Hinton once described his parents this way. "Although born in slavery and without formal education, they recognized and practiced not only the highest ideals in their personal conduct, but also the true democratic principle of equal opportunity for all, without regard to racial or religious origins or to economic or political status."

By the time he was 16, Hinton had completed his high school studies with excellence and was off to the University of Kansas in 1900. His interest in medicine was sparked by his biology teacher, but in 1902 Hinton had to drop out of college for lack of money. He worked for a year to earn money so he could return to school. During the year he was away, the University of Kansas changed its program of studies. So, in 1903 Hinton transferred to Harvard College in Cambridge, Massachusetts, where he graduated in 1905, determined on a career in medicine.

Again, lacking money, he could not enter medical school right away. Instead, he spent the next four years teaching biology, chemistry and physics at colleges in Tennessee and Oklahoma, and teaching embryology at Meharry Medical College. At the Agricultural and Mechanical College in Langston, Oklahoma, he met Ada Hawes, also a young teacher, who became Hinton's wife and a strong supporter of his work in medicine.

Throughout his teaching years, Hinton never lost sight of his goal of becoming a doctor. During the summers he continued his instruction in medicine by studying bacteriology and physiology at the University of Chicago. He was always preparing himself for the future.

In 1909 William Hinton was back in Boston as a member of the entering class of Harvard Medical School.

Despite his four-year absence from full-time study, Hinton moved through the medical school course quickly with high grades. He won the Wigglesworth Scholarship two years in a row. He refused to accept the Hayden Scholarship established for black students because he wanted to be rewarded on his merit, not compensated because of his race. Hinton supported himself and his wife by assisting Dr. Richard C. Cabot and Dr. Elmer E. Southard. Both were outstanding Harvard Medical instructors, and both were sources of inspiration to him. Dr. Southard was so impressed by Hinton's knowledge of syphilis that he arranged for him to begin teaching at the medical school about the laboratory detection of syphilis.

Hinton's life in medical school was not free from racial discrimination. Medical students received bedside instruction at Boston Lying-In Hospital. Hinton and his instructors were concerned that he, being black, would not be accepted by the patients. As it turned out, however, his presence was accepted by most patients, but fellow medical students, who had been assigned to work with him, refused to do so.

In 1912, after three years of study, Dr. Hinton graduated with honors from Harvard Medical School. It usually took four years to complete the work he had accomplished in three, but despite his successful record as a medical student his future was uncertain. All medical school graduates had to go through a period of training or an internship in a hospital. But Boston hospitals would not accept black doctors as interns.

Dr. Cabot, with whom Hinton had worked and studied, said in 1928, "But for his courage, determination and perseverance, his contributions to humanity might have been lost. He was determined to succeed without benefit of an internship which is considered essential for every doctor."

In 1912 Hinton began working each morning as a volunteer assistant in the Department of Pathology of Massachusetts

General Hospital. In the afternoons he worked as a paid assistant in the Wassermann Laboratory of the Harvard Medical School. Unable to treat patients in Boston hospitals, he turned to studying the blood serum from some of these patients.

At the Wassermann Laboratory, human blood samples were studied to detect and diagnose certain diseases, including syphilis. The laboratory, a state laboratory based at Harvard Medical School, was named for the man who devised the first test for syphilis in 1906. Hinton experienced firsthand the weaknesses and limitations of the Wassermann test. The test sometimes showed positive results when the patient wasn't infected with the syphilis germ (false positive), and some doctors were beginning to loose faith in the Wassermann test. Dr. Hinton began working to design a better test.

In 1915, the Wassermann Laboratory was transferred from Harvard University to the Massachusetts Department of Public Health. Dr. Hinton was appointed Director of the Laboratory, a position he held for 38 years. For the next 12 years he immersed himself totally in investigating a new and better test for syphilis.

In 1916, a young high school graduate, Genevieve Stuart, was appointed to the Wassermann Laboratory as a secretary to Dr. Hinton. For the remainder of her professional life she worked closely beside the black doctor who was to obtain national and international fame. After two years of typing, filing, answering the phones and keeping records for Dr. Hinton, Ms. Stuart began learning lab techniques from Dr. Hinton. She began with blood tests for syphilis and advanced to learn all the lab procedures. She remained Dr. Hinton's assistant for nearly 40 years.

When interviewed at the age of 78, Ms. Stuart remembers the early days in Dr. Hinton's lab this way: "When I went into the laboratory end of it, he was a very patient teacher. He taught most of the people who came to work at the laboratory. We were doing 100 Wassermann tests a day and also diagnosing animal heads for rabies. If you didn't have 'brains' according to him, he just didn't want you in the lab. Dr. Hinton was very fussy about how things were done. He was a perfectionist."

There were really only two worlds in Dr. Hinton's life after 1915. His laboratory was one, and his home in Canton, Massachusetts, 20 miles south of Boston, the other. The Hintons had lived in Cambridge since Dr. Hinton's medical school days, but the place there was just too small. So, in 1916 they had bought a house on four acres of land in Canton. They had never seen the inside of the house before they bought it. "The house isn't worth anything," the owner had told them. "What you're getting is the land."

When the Hinton's took over, the tiny house was in shambles. The walls were covered with bugs. It was more like a shack then anything else, but the Hinton's had dreams for their newly acquired home and land. On week-ends and during each vacation, repairs and improvements were made—several rooms and a porch were added. The tool shed, barn and garage each represented a vacation's work. Flowers, fruit trees and a lily pond surrounded the home after a few years. The Hinton's had rebuilt and replanted the place with their own hands. "I'm really just as concerned about the Japanese beetles and other bugs that eat my roses as I am about those that I find in my laboratory microscope," Dr. Hinton once observed.

*Dr. Hinton relaxing
in the garden of his home
in Canton, Massachusetts.*

When Dr. Hinton wasn't working on his home, he was at his laboratory—which was most of the time. In addition to the Wassermann Laboratory, he was also the Director of the Laboratory Department of the Boston Dispensary, a position he had also assumed in 1915. He spent his mornings at the Dispensary and afternoons at the Wassermann Laboratory. Saturdays were not a part of the weekend, but full work days for Dr. Hinton and his staff. In 1919 he received an appointment as Instructor in Preventive Medicine and Hygiene at the Harvard Medical School. That appointment marked the beginning of a 34-year teaching career at Harvard.

Dr. Hinton proved to be not only an outstanding researcher and laboratory director, but also an inspiring teacher. Ms. Stuart recalls, "The students all loved him." His manner of teaching was easy and informal—friendly, humorous and appealing. His lectures at the Medical School often ended with spontaneous applause by the students.

In 1931 his interest in training people for careers in medical science was still strong. At the Boston Dispensary Hinton started a school for training poor girls to become laboratory technicians. These classes of volunteers grew into one of the country's leading schools for preparing medical technicians.

His graduates were quickly hired by hospitals and laboratories throughout the country. The Hinton Program was a first in the country to help meet the growing demand for technicians well versed in new laboratory techniques. The program survives today as part of a training program at Northeastern University in Boston. Dr. Hinton encouraged women to become medical technicians at a time when women were not readily accepted in the medical world.

Meanwhile, he carried on his research in the pathology of venereal diseases. Blood serum, test tubes and chemicals from sick and healthy patients occupied more and more of his time. Lunch hours were spent in the laboratory. "All I ever saw him with was a cup of coffee," recalled Ms. Stuart. While carrying out his research, Hinton was responsible for all the syphilis testing done in Massachusetts, and he had taken over all the rabies work for the State Division of Animal Husbandry. When the state began requiring blood tests of couples before marriage and of mothers before the birth of babies, Dr. Hinton supervised the expansion of the state laboratory facilities—at the time of his appointment there had been ten state laboratories. He increased the number to 117. In addition, his laboratory was conducting research on tuberculosis and influenza.

Hinton's single, most important contribution to medicine, however, was his work with syphilis. Just two years after his medical school graduation, he had published his first scientific paper on the serology of syphilis. His understanding of the disease was so comprehensive that he was asked to write the definitive chapter on syphilis for the *Textbook of Preventive Medicine*.

By 1927, Hinton had developed and perfected his blood serum test for syphilis.

After 12 years of painstaking laboratory work, the Hinton Test was rated outstanding both because of its sensitivity and specificity. Hinton's method drastically reduced the large number of false-positive results given by the Wassermann method. Because treatment of syphilis at that time was so long, painful and dangerous, and the stigma of venereal disease so dreaded, an accurate test was of utmost importance.

The Hinton Test was a floculation test. A sample of the liquid portion of a patient's blood, called serum, was combined in a test tube with a mixture of glycerine solution, sodium chloride and a substance prepared from powdered beef heart muscle. The tube was shaken vigorously for three minutes to mix the serum with the other substances and then placed overnight in a warm water bath. In the morning the tube was held up to a bright light and examined for a whitish ring of particles at the top of the fluid. If the coarse particles appeared, the test was positive; the patient was carrying the syphilis germ. If there were no white particles, the test was negative; the patient was not syphilitic.

Hinton's test was 98% accurate, but Hinton wasn't completely satisfied, and he worked four more years perfecting his technique. It was the most delicate and sensitive test ever designed to diagnose syphilis. It seldom gave a positive result with blood serum from a person not infected with syphilis. By 1931 he had developed an improved test which could be done with smaller amounts of blood. Dr. John Davies had worked along with Hinton in the modification of the test, and it became known as the Hinton-Davies Test. It was adopted as the official test of the Massachusetts Department of Public Health in its state lab in 1935. Outside of Massachusetts the test became widely known and used for more than 20 years.

While Hinton's laboratory gained prominence and commanded much of his time, he could still escape to Canton. On many a summer day his laboratories would be decorated with flowers from his garden; his staff and colleagues at the Medical School would enjoy the vegetables grown by Hinton and his wife. Ada Hinton was really the gardner. She constantly had her hands and knees in the soil. Her husband loved the final products and made sure that his orchard and gardens had every possible variety of plant that would grow in New England.

Corn, beans and tomatoes were grown each summer. Dr. Hinton was proud of the beans, and one day had picked a large bag to share with the doctors at the Medical School. But his wife Ada said, "No, I raised those beans." She had nurtured them from seedlings.

Most of the furniture and cabinetry inside the Hinton home had been built by the doctor himself. He was an expert cabinetmaker. He loved antiques, and Sunday afternoon drives with his wife and two daughters often included visits to antique shops in the Boston area.

Despite his interests at home, Dr. Hinton was restless. He was always getting back to his laboratory and his test tubes, leaving household management to his wife. He was a completely dedicated scientist—his medical work came first.

Ada Hinton seldom visited her husband's laboratory. When she did it was to join him for the ride home to Canton at the end of his day. In addition to raising their two daughters,

Mrs. Hinton spent much time in Boston working at Massachusetts General Hospital in the field of medical social work. She served as the vice-president of the Boston Housing Foundation, president of the Community Fund in Canton and vice-president of the Home for Aged Colored Women in Boston. Today, in Boston's black community of Roxbury, there is a housing development for the elderly known as the Ada Hinton Homes in her memory.

In 1934, Dr. Hinton began writing his classic text *Syphilis and Its Treatment*. For two years, the writing of the book was a night and day passion for Gus and Ada Hinton. Mrs. Hinton was as much a driving force behind the book as was her husband. She gave him great moral support and took over all household chores caring for their Canton estate so that he could devote his full time and energy to writing.

Dr. Hinton tried to provide "a clear, simple, relatively complete account of syphilis and its treatment for physicians, public health workers and medical students." The book was warmly received upon publication in 1936. It was studied in Europe and the United States as a unique contribution to the field of venereal disease. Encompassing Hinton's 20 years of research in the laboratory and hospital clinic, the book became a standard reference source in medical schools and hospitals.

Dr. Hinton made it very clear that diseases such as syphilis were "a by-product of poverty and ignorance and poor living conditions . . . that race was not the determining factor, but that it was, rather the socioeconomic condition of the patient." He felt syphilis was a disease of the underprivileged. His book documented his years of research and "his experience in clinics with patients and the disease from their point of view."

Just as his celebrated test for syphilis was a milestone in helping to conquer the disease, so his book was a milestone in medical writing on the subject.

Four years after the publication of his book, Dr. Hinton suffered an automobile accident that tragically changed the course of his life. The roads from his home in Canton to his laboratory at Harvard were icy on a cold November morning in 1940. As he drove alone to work that day, his car skidded on the icy pavement and slammed into a stone wall in Boston's Jamaica Plain section. Dr. Hinton climbed from his wrecked automobile and was hit and dragged along the road by another car. His right leg was badly damaged, and he was taken to the emergency ward at Boston's Peter Bent Brigham Hospital. Infection set in, and amputation of the leg was the only way to save Hinton's life. The loss of his right leg caused him chronic pain until his death, 19 years later. Despite his handicap during the last years of his life, he continued to teach at Harvard Medical School, the Harvard School of Public Health and at the Boston Dispensary.

Recognition came slowly and late to Dr. Hinton. In 1946, he was promoted to the rank of Lecturer on Bacteriology and Immunology at the Harvard Medical School. And three years later, a year before he retired and 22 years after he developed his test for syphilis, Dr. Hinton was elevated to the position of Clinical Professor at Harvard—the first black person to attain the rank of Professor at Harvard.

Dr. Hinton was a modest man. Because he was so self-effacing perhaps his achievements were not as widely known as they should have been. As a young doctor he believed that it was a scientist's duty to serve humanity, that the greatest reward for long hours of work in stuffy laboratories would be discoveries that would advance human knowledge and raise health standards. He disliked publicity and refused to promote himself on the basis of his contributions to medical science. In addition to his natural modesty, he also felt that widespread knowledge that he was a black man would delay the acceptance of his test and book in the medical world. Most men interested in the field of syphilis knew that he was black, but Hinton didn't want those who didn't know his race to use color as a reason for not recognizing his accomplishments. For this reason he would not accept the Spingarn Medal from the National Association for the Advancement of Colored People in 1938 when this organization wanted to honor him. He wanted his work to be accepted on its merit alone.

Dr. Hinton's fears about his test and book not being accepted because he was black were real. Although the U.S. Public Health Service ranked his test above all others for syphilis in 1934 and the American Serology Committee praised his test for its accuracy and simplicity in 1935, there was resistance to using it in some state health departments because it had been developed by a black man.

Dr. Hinton's legacy to medicine was not forgotten. In 1974, 15 years after his death, when the State Laboratory Institute Building of the Massachusetts Department of Public Health was dedicated, the serology laboratory was named The Dr. William A. Hinton Serology Laboratory—the laboratory he had headed for 38 years and where he had carried out his research in syphilis. During his lifetime Dr. Hinton probably would not have allowed the laboratory to be named after him, but it is a proper tribute to one of America's giants of medicine.

LOUIS T. WRIGHT

1891–1952

Researcher, Surgeon, Fighter for Equality

In the summer of 1911, a young black man named Louis Wright boarded a train in Atlanta, Georgia. He was on his way to Boston to study medicine at Harvard University. Just a few weeks earlier, he had graduated from Clark College in Atlanta. But his college diploma was not the only preparation for his medical education. As the train sped north, Louis Wright carried with him memories and experiences that would eventually produce a dedicated researcher and physician, and a tough-minded fighter for the right of black people to good medical care.

As a boy growing up in Atlanta, Louis Wright had seen racial injustice firsthand. He remembered the chain gangs of black prisoners who had built many of Atlanta's streets. The memory of the beatings and name calling against those shackled and sweating men never left him.

When Louis was 15, a race riot broke out in Atlanta. His stepfather gave Louis a loaded Winchester rifle and said "Son, you cover the front of the house. If anybody comes in that gate, let 'em have it. If you see they're going to get you, try to take two of them with you."

Louis was really frightened. But he took his post in the front of the house. As the night wore on, he heard gunfire in the distance. In the bright moonlight he could see the militia marching up the road in front of the house. He saw his white neighbors take their guns and march up the road. Louis realized that he and his stepfather could not defend their home all by themselves. But he stood his ground at the front window. "Once you've faced death, you don't fear anything," he said later.

The family was saved by a white auto mechanic who drove

them to a safer part of town. Thus Louis learned an important thing. He learned not to judge people by their blackness or whiteness. It was a belief that sometimes made enemies for him among black people in the years to come.

Louis knew what it was to be a physician. His stepfather, Dr. William Fletcher Penn, was a physician. Louis knew the step of the anxious father on the porch when a baby was due. He knew the worry Dr. Penn felt as he nursed many people through a diphtheria epidemic. And Louis saw the joy when a baby was born and the sadness when a patient died. He knew he wanted to be a physician.

No one would ever tell Louis Wright he couldn't find a way to use these memories and experiences. He believed in himself, perhaps more so because there were those around him who did not think black people could accomplish worthwhile things. That belief met its first major test at Harvard University.

The Harvard admissions office was more than a little surprised to find that one of their applicants was a graduate of Clark University in Atlanta. To them it was one of those "funny little schools" which they felt certain could not prepare a person to enter Harvard Medical School. Not only that but Louis Wright had not taken his chemistry exam. The admissions office sent Wright to the office of Dr. Otto Folin, a Harvard professor and famous chemist. Quite a heated discussion took place in Dr. Folin's office. Louis Wright insisted that he be permitted to study medicine at Harvard. Dr. Folin insisted that he felt Louis wasn't prepared for the study of medicine.

Finally Dr. Folin said, "Will you agree that if I ask you a

few questions here today, I will never be bothered with you again in life?''

Wright agreed.

Dr. Folin then gave Wright an oral chemistry quiz. Wright passed successfully and was admitted to Harvard.

Louis Wright did well at Harvard, making such good grades that he won a scholarship each year. In the beginning of his third year he faced his next big hurdle. It is in the third year that medical students begin to do actual work with patients. When the assignments were given out, Wright was told that he could not go with his classmates to Boston Lying-In Hospital to learn to deliver babies (obstetrics). He would have to learn obstetrics under a black Harvard graduate who practiced in Boston. "That is the way all the colored men get their obstetrics," said the instructor.

"I paid my tuition," said Wright. "And I want what the catalog calls for, namely obstetrics at Boston Lying-In."

Wright got what the catalog called for and thus ended one kind of discrimination.

Wright was a senior at Harvard when he took a big chance with all he had worked so hard for. The movie, *The Birth of a Nation*, was playing at the Tremont Theatre during the spring of 1915. It was considered by black people and some whites to be a racist, anti-black film. It gave an unfair picture of black Americans in the South after the Civil War.

Louis Wright joined the fight to have the showing of the film stopped. For three weeks he cut classes and took time from his studying to march in the picket line in front of the theatre in protest.

The pressure brought by the protesters resulted in a law

that set up a film censorship board that could ban improper films. The board did not ban *The Birth of a Nation* after reviewing it. Although the black citizens of Boston were not successful in driving the film out of Boston, it was the first time that blacks and whites in Boston had worked together for respect and justice for black people.

The day after the governor signed the censorship board bill, Wright returned to class. When he told his professor where he had been, the professor said, "I don't blame you. I think that's more important than your having been in my classes."

Louis Wright graduated fourth in his class at Harvard Medical School in 1915. Now he needed to find a hospital where he could serve his internship, a year of practical hospital work that is required before a medical graduate can be licensed to practice.

Here again Louis Wright faced the problem of color. "We've not taken Negro nurses, and we're not going to take Negro doctors," they said at one Massachusetts hospital.

"We've got troubles enough without adding the race problem," was another reply.

Louis Wright tried the hospitals in Canada. From Vancouver General Hospital in British Columbia came this refusal. "I have no doubt in the world but what you would make an excellent intern in our hospital, but on account of your being a colored man I would be unable to take you on the staff."

Finally Wright's stepfather suggested that he try Freedman's Hospital in Washington, D.C. Freedman's was the teaching hospital for Howard University, a black university.

Dr. Wright was accepted at Freedman's and began his internship. It was at Freedman's that Dr. Wright began his first piece of research. He had gotten a taste of research at Harvard while studying the effect of alcohol on the function of the stomach.

One of the major health problems of the day was diphtheria. Diphtheria is a throat infection that can be fatal. The key to treating this contagious disease lies in prevention, that is, in giving susceptible persons a protective injection. Just two years earlier, in 1913, a Hungarian pediatrician, Dr. Bela Schick, had perfected a way of determining susceptibility to diphtheria. The test involved injecting a few drops of the diphtheria bacterium's poison or toxin into the skin. If the injected area became red and swollen after a few days and then turned brown, the doctor knew that the person lacked immunity to diphtheria. The test is called the Schick test.

In medical school Dr. Wright had been taught that blacks are more susceptible to diphtheria than whites. Dr. Wright had also read that the Schick test was of little or no use in black people since it could not be read on brown skin.

A diphtheria epidemic among doctors, nurses and patients at Freedman's spurred Dr. Wright to put those two theories to the test. In his experiment, Dr. Wright gave the Schick test to 207 black people and three white people. Skin color ranged from white to light brown to dark brown.

After a few days, Dr. Wright could see that the Schick test did work on black people. While he couldn't always see the redness, there were other definite signs. The injected area became slightly swollen and the normally spiderylike lines of the skin grew thick and more definite. Silvery white scales formed in the area. Next the area got darker than the surrounding area. On fair skin, the area turned light brown. On brown skins, the area turned black. And less than half of the black people tested proved to be susceptible to diphtheria, which is also the average for white people.

Dr. Wright had made his first important contribution to medical knowledge. He wrote a report on his research and sent it to the *Journal of Infectious Diseases*. It was the first published research to come from Freedman's Hospital. Other medical journals, as well as textbook authors, quoted Dr. Wright's results.

But Dr. Wright didn't exactly cover himself with glory at Freedman's. He was forever telling off some white person whom he thought was insulting a black person. Once he told a United States Senator not to call him "Sam". "It's time you learned to call a doctor a doctor," Dr. Wright said to the Senator. On another occasion he told the Commissioner of Health to remove his hat in the women's ward. "You're the Commissioner of Health, and you should certainly know better," said Dr. Wright.

Although the superintendent of the hospital cringed from fear of his white budget controllers, he stood behind Dr. Wright.

When Dr. Wright had finished his internship, he took the examination for his license to practice medicine, making the very highest scores. As a licensed physician, Dr. Wright went back to Atlanta to work with his stepfather. In Atlanta something happened which brought him face to face with a frightening part of himself.

The incident happened at the courthouse in Atlanta. Dr. Wright had gone there to register his medical license. An elderly white man took his license and told him to sit on the bench. As Dr. Wright sat waiting, he suddenly heard someone call "Louie! Louie!" Dr. Wright didn't answer. Then the man came over and kicked his foot.

"I was talking to you," the man said.

"You're not talking to me. I'm Dr. Louis T. Wright," said Dr. Wright.

Next the man called, "Wright! Wright!" Again Dr. Wright told him his name.

"You aren't going to sell any dope are you?" asked the man.

"Let me tell you something! I'll choke you right here if you open your mouth again." At that moment, Dr. Wright really believed himself capable of violence. He simply could not swallow the disrespect this man was showing him. Realizing how angry Dr. Wright was, the man quickly gave him his certificate.

Dr. Wright went home and told his parents what had happened. He was certain that it would be better for him to leave Atlanta to avoid landing in jail. He had learned that there were certain insults he couldn't accept. He was horrified at the depth of his anger and did not sleep for three nights.

In the end, Dr. Wright remained in Atlanta, for his stepfather needed him in the office.

Perhaps it was in Atlanta that Dr. Wright reached the depths of his bitterness over the bad treatment of blacks by whites. In later years, Dr. Wright's wife was to describe this bitterness as she saw it in her husband.

"He had the same amount of bitterness that lots of people in the Negro race have, but he got over it in later life. He would say to me, 'Bitterness doesn't pay. It frustrates your efforts to do things. It cuts your efficiency. Therefore it is an evil thing. It is a destructive force.' "

It was while he was in Atlanta working with his stepfather that Dr. Wright began to pursue his special interest in surgery. He was appointed surgeon to Clark University, his old school. He did his surgery at Fairhaven Infirmary in Atlanta.

The year was 1917. Dr. Wright was scarcely in Atlanta a year when the United States declared war on Germany. With the entry of his country into World War I, Dr. Wright joined the army. He was commissioned a first lieutenant and sent to Medical Officers Training Camp in Des Moines, Iowa.

After basic training, Lt. Wright was sent to Camp Upton, New York. He found medical work in an army camp decidedly monotonous. It meant examining feet, making sure the garbage was removed, and vaccinating all the men.

But he quickly found a way to make it interesting.

Lt. Wright was having trouble vaccinating the men against smallpox. When a doctor vaccinates a person against smallpox, he innoculates a virus in between the skin layers. He then looks for a "take" as an indication that the person has been made immune to the disease. The "take" is signaled by the appearance of tiny reddish pimples at the innoculated spot on the arm. These tiny pimples get bigger and then break open and dry up. A scab forms which eventually falls off, leaving a scar.

In 1917, there were three methods of placing the virus in between the layers of the skin. All three involved puncturing or scratching the skin of the arm and then rubbing the virus into the tiny wound. Lt. Wright was using the official army method of rubbing the virus into two scratches made with a

sterile needle. But he was getting few "takes," even after re-
peating the vaccination many times.

Wasn't there a better way to innoculate the virus into the
skin layers, he wondered. Then he thought of injecting the
virus into the skin, intradermal or intracutaneous it was called.
It was much the same way he had injected the toxin in his
Schick test research.

Selecting 227 volunteers, who had shown no "takes," Lt.
Wright tried out his new idea. On each man's arm he tried the
official army scratch method and his new injection method.
Out of 227 men, 160 had "takes" with the new injection
method. But only 19 had "takes" with the scratch method.

Lt. Wright's new method seemed a much better way to vac-
cinate against smallpox. He reported the results to his com-
manding officer. The army immediately made Wright's
method the official army method of vaccination. And Lt.
Wright was recommended for promotion to captain. He passed
his promotion exam with a perfect score. But his promotion
was blocked throughout the war by a lieutenant colonel who
refused to approve it.

It was in New York that Dr. Wright met Miss Corrine
Cooke, the woman he was later to marry. His wife remembers
their first meeting very well. She says, "I met Louis, who was
very shy, when I was selling tickets to raise money for an army
dance. He had watched me work and was impressed with what
I was doing. He loved efficiency."

In June, 1918, Lt. Wright landed with his regiment in
France. Although he did not wear captain's bars, he was
given the duties of a captain. He was made battalion surgeon
and was put in charge of the surgical wards.

He escaped the German bullets, but Lt. Wright was caught in a poison gas attack. It put him in the hospital for three weeks. Afterward he returned to his regiment, but the lingering damage to his lungs was to trouble him for the rest of his life.

On the day the war ended, November 11, 1918, the officer who had opposed Lt. Wright's promotion was transferred. And three hours after the officer left, his replacement signed Lt. Wright's promotion papers.

When he returned to the United States, Dr. Wright decided to settle in New York City. He now had a wife and small daughter. Once he had found a home and office, he decided to seek a position on the staff of a New York hospital. He filed his application with the New York Board of Hospitals. For years, black doctors had tried for staff positions in the New York hospitals without success. When they filed their applications, they were told, "We'll let you know when there's a vacancy." But somehow there never seemed to be a vacancy.

Every day Dr. Wright appeared at the board offices to check on vacancies. Each day, the answer was "You'll be notified, Dr. Wright." This went on for six months; it might have gone on for much longer had Dr. Wright not happened to meet Dr. Cosmo O'Neal, superintendent of Harlem Hospital.

Dr. O'Neal knew of Dr. Wright's work with the Schick test and smallpox vaccination. "I wish we could get a man like you in our out-patient department," he said.

"Have you got a vacancy?" asked Dr. Wright.

"We've been pitifully understaffed ever since the war," said Dr. O'Neal.

"Won't the board be glad to get this news? They've been looking for a vacancy for me," said Dr. Wright.

"You would consider it?" said Dr. O'Neal. "When could you come?"

"When? Tomorrow morning," said Dr. Wright.

And so Dr. Wright became the first black doctor to be appointed to the staff of a New York hospital. The next day when he reported for duty, four staff physicians walked out. Two days later, Dr. O'Neal was transferred from the Harlem Hospital superintendency to Bellevue Hospital garbage inspectorship.

The barriers to black physicians had been broken. And four more black doctors joined the Harlem Hospital staff. But the battle was not over. When the black doctors came up for promotion, they were told by the hospital board that blacks could not be promoted. And any doctor who did not like the situation was invited to resign.

Dr. Wright did not resign. Instead he renewed his fight. He had not forgotten his friend Dr. O'Neal. He wanted to get justice for him as well as for black physicians. Dr. Wright rallied his friends to fight the hospital board's policy.

News of the battle at Harlem Hospital got into *The New York News,* a black newspaper. Black newspapers in other parts of the country picked up the story. People began to ask the mayor of New York City what he was going to do about the Harlem Hospital situation. The National Association for the Advancement of Colored People (NAACP), of which Dr. Wright was a member, supported his battle. Dr. Wright's friend, City Commissioner Ferdinand Morton used his influence with the mayor. Finally, the mayor launched an investigation of the hospital board.

As a result, the head of the hospital board was fired. The

hospital was declared open to all qualified physicians, no matter what color. And Dr. Cosmo O'Neal was transferred from the Bellevue garbage yard to the superintendency of Fordham Hospital.

Dr. Wright was appointed to the surgical staff at Harlem Hospital. Now he was able to build his skill as a surgeon. In 1929, he was appointed a New York City police surgeon, another first for a black physician.

In 1931, Dr. Wright found another battle to fight. He learned that the Julius Rosenwald Fund, an organization that provided money for worthwhile projects, was planning to build a black hospital.

In his announcement speech, Mr. Edwin Embree, president of the Fund, said that the hospital was needed to provide training for black doctors and nurses and to make health care available to black people.

Dr. Wright fought the planned new hospital by writing an eight-page pamphlet. In the pamphlet, he pointed out that a black hospital was not the solution to the black health care problem. "A segregated hospital makes the white person feel superior and the black person feel inferior," Dr. Wright wrote. "It sets the black person apart from all other citizens as being a different kind of citizen and a different kind of medical student and physician which you know and we know is not the case. What the Negro physician needs is equal opportunity for training and practice — no more, no less. Sick Negroes require exactly the same care as do other sick people. Segregated hospitals are always neglected. They represent a duality of citizenship in a democratic government that is wrong."

The pamphlet struck a fatal blow against the project. Not

only was the hospital not built but other "black-only" hospitals being planned were not built.

That battle won, Dr. Wright turned his attention to treating the injuries that filled the surgical wards of Harlem Hospital.

Gunshot wounds were becoming a more frequent problem for Harlem Hospital. With each new case, Dr. Wright learned more. He learned how to tell the path of the bullet by studying the wound. He learned the value of restoring lost blood with intravenous fluids. And when surgery was necessary to repair the damage done by the bullet. Dr. Wright found it best to make a large incision so that he could make certain he had not missed any damage done by the bullet.

Another problem that needed solving was how to handle the patient with a broken or dislocated neck. Moving the person after the injury could cause the damaged bones to injure the spinal cord, possibly causing paralysis. Dr. Wright could see that what was needed was a brace. But none seemed to exist. And so Dr. Wright invented one. He needed a good way to treat severe fractures of the leg. And so he invented a special metal plate for splinting such injuries. Dr. Wright became such an expert on bone injuries that he was asked to write a chapter in a medical book about bone injuries.

Dr. Wright was still paying the bills for building the models for the neck brace when he became very ill. A lung hemorrhage sent him to the hospital. His lungs, weakened by the gas attack during the war, had now become infected with tuberculosis. For nine months, he lay on his side in the hospital. To build up his weakened body, he was given a rich diet of beef, milk and cream.

After a year he began to lose hope that he would ever get

well. He became frightened. He wanted to live. There was so much more he wanted to do. Dr. Wright's doctor felt that a change of scene would probably help. And so Dr. Wright was moved to a hospital in Ithaca, New York. There in a room with a view of a lake, Dr. Wright's hope began to grow. His family, and patients as well, made frequent trips to Ithaca. Finally after three years at Ithaca, Dr. Wright went home on a stretcher.

His heart had been permanently damaged by his long illness. His doctor had given him many rules to follow—no stairs and daily naps. He was not permitted to do surgery since the gases used for anesthesia were harmful to his lungs.

While still flat on his back, Dr. Wright was appointed chief of surgery at Harlem Hospital. Now a new kind of life began for him. Restricted in his physical activity, he became an advisor, a teacher, a research leader.

As chief of surgery, Dr. Wright was able to take a hand in directing his dream of making Harlem Hospital truly an example of an interracial hospital. He refused to promote any physician just because he was black. "I insist on the best man for the spot, white or black, Jew or Catholic. And that's all there is to it," he often said. This policy cost him the friendship of some black physicians.

Dr. Wright insisted on the very best work from all staff members. A young white intern quickly found that out. He was not interested in surgery, and he was certain that the standards of a city hospital would not be high. He took little trouble with patient histories—brief summaries of past sicknesses the patient has had. To the intern's surprise, Dr. Wright called him into his office and said, "Young man, henceforth you will write medical school histories. Now is that clear to you?''

For those whom he had to correct, Dr. Wright often had this advice, ''Accept your punishment and go ahead and learn from it.''

Dr. Wright set up a five year surgery training program at Harlem Hospital. Then he urged young interns to study surgery. Somehow he managed to send the spark that had spurred his own ambition across the desk to many a young intern.

It was during this time that Dr. Wright did most of his research. Such research involved everything from new ways to do certain kinds of surgery to the dangerous side-effects of a certain medicine.

Perhaps his most important research involved the first tests on humans of the antibiotic, aureomycin. An antibiotic is a substance produced by a mold which will kill certain disease organisms. Aureomycin had been tried on laboratory mice but never on humans. Dr. Wright tested aureomycin on the victims of a virus disease for which there was no known treatment. The patients were helped by the new antibiotic.

The year was 1949, only a few years after the miracle antibiotic, penicillin, had come into use. Now it seemed that aureomycin might be the new *wonder* antibiotic. Dr. Wright and other scientists did more tests with the new antibiotic. It was found to cure such diseases as pneumonia, intestinal infections, typhus and certain infections that sometimes followed surgery.

Cancer research was another important project begun by Dr. Wright in 1948. He began to look for chemicals that would kill cancer cells without killing the cancer victim. He organized the Harlem Hospital Cancer Research Foundation. By now his daughters were grown and had become physicians. Dr. Barbara Wright and Dr. Jane Wright joined their father in his cancer research.

In April, 1952, Harlem Hospital honored Dr. Wright by naming the new medical library after him. At the dedication ceremonies, Dr. Wright said, "Harlem Hospital represents the finest example of democracy at work in the field of medicine. Its policy of complete integration throughout the institution has stood the test of time."

It was an announcement that an important dream had been accomplished. Now he could devote most of his time to research. But it was not to be. For there was not much time left for Dr. Wright. In October, 1952, his heart failed and he died. He left much behind—better medical care for many, more opportunities for black physicians, and a daughter, Dr. Jane Wright, who would carry on his cancer research.

WILLIAM MONTAGUE COBB

1904–

Anatomist, Teacher, Editor

The book is tattered and worn. A piece of white string holds the pages within the binding. The once green binding is now gray and scuffed. A dim glint reveals the gold lettering on the book, *The Animal Kingdom, Illustrated* by S.G. Goodrich. It is the treasured possession of Dr. William Montague Cobb. Dr. Cobb carefully unties the string to reveal the faded inscription inside the cover. "This was given to my great-grandmother by my great-grandfather in 1871," he says.

The pages of the book are filled with complete descriptions of all animals, including man. Detailed drawings, show what many of the animals look like. "My interest in animals began with this book," says Dr. Cobb. From a small boy interested in animals has grown a man who is anatomist, physician, teacher, writer and activist for the rights of black people.

Montague Cobb's native city of Washington, D.C., was full of experiences to learn from. "We were poor, but I didn't feel deprived," he often says. Washington offered free concerts, zoos, galleries and aquariums. To get to those things, Montague and his friends found that long hikes around Washington were often necessary. Those long hikes conditioned the future distance runner who was destined to break several records in college. Free concerts by the Marine Band gave the boy an ear for music that later spurred the man to play the violin in his leisure.

The zoo visits are his most vivid memories. His favorite animal was the rhino. To him the rhino was totally amazing. "It was an animal with tremendous tonnage. I knew that the skull itself weighed over 100 pounds. And it could move at speeds of 40 miles per hour. And yet, with all that weight, the rhino had control. That was really anatomy in action."

On other occasions, the boy would visit the Natural History Museum. He would stare up at the skeletons of the dinosaurs and wonder why those animals had been unsuccessful experiments and become extinct. And the eohippus—that tiny ancestor of the horse—why had it galloped off into extinction?

Montague was bright, and that got him in trouble. When he skipped a grade in elementary school, he found himself the smallest boy in the sixth grade.

"I lost a lot of fights that year," he remembers. He sent away for a book on boxing. During the summer, he used the book as a guide and taught himself to box. As he began his seventh grade classes, the bullies descended upon him again. But this time, he was ready for them. He threw a few of his newly-learned punches at one of the bullies. And things settled down.

At Dunbar High School, Montague Cobb became a star athlete, winning two varsity letters in track and cross-country, and a scholarship to Amherst College in Amherst, Massachusetts. At Amherst, he continued to make a name for himself in track. He won the intramural cross-country championship three years in a row. Montague also found some use for his seventh grade boxing skills at Amherst, where he won the lightweight and welterweight titles.

Upon graduation from Amherst, he was awarded the Blodgett scholarship for proficiency in biology. The scholarship meant spending a summer at the Marine Biological Laboratory in Woods Hole, Massachusetts. Important research on marine animals was being done at the Institute.

Montague Cobb recalls the Woods Hole summer as his happiest. He studied embryology, the growth and development of such animals as round worms and jelly fish, and attended lectures by famous scientists. Each morning, the students went out on the Woods Hole yacht and caught the specimens they needed. Then they studied the eggs and embryos under the microscopes. Montague filled a thick notebook with sketches and descriptions of what he saw. Finely detailed sketches showed, for example, the various changes which a fertilized egg undergoes. Patiently the student had watched the changing egg through the lens of his microscope, drawing and describing those changes as they occurred. In another series, a microscopic view of a tiny fish was captured by Montague's pen. Each blood vessel and turn of the digestive tract is carefully drawn. He received a certificate in embryology for his work at Woods Hole. But far more important to Montague was his newly-gained skill as a laboratory biologist. He truly felt that now he was on his way to become a student of living things.

That fall, Montague Cobb enrolled in the Howard Medical School in Washington, D.C. He did so well in medical school that, by his senior year, he was appointed an instructor in embryology. Then followed a year's internship at Freedman's Hospital. There he learned that an understanding of biology was not the only necessity for treating patients. He began to see that a doctor had to combine his understanding of medicine with an understanding of people. One patient he was treating was very fat. In an effort to help her lose weight, Dr. Cobb prescribed a customary daily dose of magnesium sulfate, a laxative, also called epsom salts. After a few doses of that, the patient told Dr. Cobb one day that she couldn't stand any more of that medicine. He decided to try a dose of epsom salts himself. It was so terrible that he canceled the laxative order. From then on he often tried some of the less harmful medications on himself before he prescribed them.

Dr. Cobb had intended to begin practicing medicine when he finished his internship for he now had a wife and small daughter. But the doctor was urged by Dr. Numa Adams, Howard Medical School dean, to spend several years studying anatomy with Dr. Thomas Wingate Todd. Dr. Todd was Professor of Anatomy at Western Reserve University in Cleveland, Ohio.

Under Dr. Todd's guidance, Dr. Cobb developed a view of anatomy that would guide his entire future career. Dr. Todd rejected the idea that anatomy was the mere memorizing of body parts. He believed that anatomy, since it dealt with the structure of the organism, was the basic biological science. Physiology was simply anatomy in action, pathology (study of disease) was abnormal anatomy, and biochemistry just microscopic anatomy.

In 1932, after receiving his Ph.D. in anatomy and physical anthropology, Dr. Cobb returned to Howard University Medical School where he joined the Department of Anatomy as an assistant professor.

Like many good anatomy professors, Dr. Cobb began his teaching career with a simple goal in mind. Since anatomy was the basic science for physicians, he wanted his students to master it as they would any other skill. Anatomy should be as automatic as driving a car or playing a musical instrument. Without hesitation, they should know the structures of their patient's body.

Dr. Cobb felt that the mere memorizing of the names of

muscles and bones and other structures was not the best way to achieve this goal. The student needed to understand how a muscle, for example, fitted into the organization of bodily functions. It was not enough to memorize the bones in the arch of the foot. How much better to approach the problem as one of mechanics. How does the arch function? What moves it? What supports it?

But by far the most important contribution to the teaching of anatomy by Dr. Montague Cobb was what he invented and called the *Roentgenoscopic (X ray) eye*. The X ray eye enabled the student to learn anatomy from the skin in. Thus, the student would be able to look at a certain point on the patient's body and visualize the structures beneath the skin.

The two basic teaching tools used in helping students to acquire an X ray eye were a human skeleton and a human cadaver (dead person). The cadaver was propped up alongside the skeleton. Then one of the students stripped off his shirt and stood next to the cadaver. By studying the bones of the skeleton and the structures inside the cadaver, the students outlined the structures of such organs as the heart and the lungs on the skin of their classmate. Mimeographed outlines of the body provided further practice toward training the X ray eye. The students were learning living anatomy instead of the dead anatomy found by simply dissecting a cadaver.

Once his students had mastered the X ray eye, Dr. Cobb taught them to draw the body. He offered them an easy guide for getting the body proportions correct. The unit of measure is the head. The body should be seven and one half heads high. The hipbone is the middle of the body. The nipples are two heads from the top and one head apart. The navel is three

Dr. Montague Cobb with his vast collection of human skulls.

heads from the top. With those measurements as guides, students easily added the other features such as arms and legs.

"No need to be an artist," Dr. Cobb told his students, "All you need is knowledge." He believed that drawing the structures was the best way to understand and become familiar with them. "Drawing," he said, "will also help you to find weak points or gaps in your knowledge of anatomy."

Dr. Cobb called his new method of teaching anatomy the "graphic method of anatomy." The new method received a commendation from the National Medical Association. A fellow anatomy professor at Howard called Dr. Cobb "a great classical anatomist." "The more I listened to him, the more I learned," he said. But perhaps the highest praise of Cobb, the teacher, could be found in the jammed lecture hall. Students, not even enrolled in medical school, often came to hear his lectures on anatomy.

In addition to his new teaching method, Dr. Cobb made many other contributions to the Department of Anatomy at

Howard. He began an anatomical museum which included examples of many features such as skull shapes and breathing apparatus. He assembled a collection of over 600 human and animal skeletons for study by many different departments in the University.

Dr. Cobb put the entire anatomy course on 8 mm movie sound film. He did all the filming and editing himself. This provided the department with another unique teaching tool. The film could serve as a review or an introduction of the anatomy course. In addition, he started to collect color slides of vital structures and microscopic views—another excellent teaching tool.

Even though he was busy teaching full time, Dr. Cobb couldn't forget those days at Woods Hole. The memory of discovering and finally understanding a biological principle never left him. And whenever he could get away to Cleveland, Dr. Cobb worked in the Western Reserve labs of his old professor, Dr. T. Wingate Todd. There a huge anatomy collection was available. There were skeletons, slides showing microscopic views of various tissues, and organs and other body parts preserved in formaldehyde.

For Dr. Cobb, the most interesting part of anatomy was the skeleton, that framework on which the body depends for support. The shapes and the fitting together of the bones fascinated him. He was certain that each shape and each fit had a purpose.

Dr. Cobb especially wondered what shaped the bones of the head. What purpose did the shape of the bones of the face serve? Why, for example, did a camel have a rounded muzzle while a tiger had scarcely any nose at all?

As a graduate student working under Dr. Todd, Dr. Cobb had concluded that the growth of the upper teeth seemed to be one major force which shaped the upper jaw and the face. He wondered how the growth of teeth produced so many differently shaped faces as occurred in mammals. He decided to study all the mammals.

Approaching the problem as an engineer might, Dr. Cobb studied the construction of 1100 mammalian skulls. As a guideline he asked himself several questions. What were the needs of the animals? How did the teeth serve those needs? How did the growth of the necessary teeth shape the animal's face?

Thus in his study, Dr. Cobb gave special attention to the rounded knobs on each side of the upper jawbone. These knobs are called maxillary tubers. It is there that the upper molars, or the grinding teeth, form. And it is the growth of that part of the bone which seemed to play a major role in shaping the face.

When Dr. Cobb examined the camel skull, he found that the maxillary tuber grew out and back towards the base of the skull. Such growth gave the tuber little support. But the jawbone (to which the tuber was attached) thickened and grew forward, thus providing a strong foundation for the tuber and the teeth that developed. Thus the camel has a rounded snout and many molars for grinding the grains and grasses it eats.

In the tiger skull, Dr. Cobb found that the maxillary tubers had grown sideways out from the head. The cheekbones and jaw joint were thickened to support powerful jaw muscles. The result was a V-shaped skull, well designed for tearing flesh.

In humans, the maxillary tuber simply attached itself to the underside of the palate bone, producing a smaller face and a set of teeth suitable for eating many different kinds of foods.

In another project at Western Reserve, Dr. Cobb studied the growth and development of the human breastbone (sternum). Working with X rays and skeletons of 1010 dead persons, Dr. Cobb found two important types of human sterna, the upward curved (convex) and the downward curved chest (concave). Tiny undeveloped bones, called ossicles, were found in many of the skeletons with convex breastbones. These ossicles (suprasternal bones) are thought to be remnants left over from earlier mammals.

Thus to Dr. Cobb, the finding of a convex sternum with the ossicles seemed to mean that he was looking at a skeleton slightly more primitive than one which did not have the ossicles. More of those supposedly primitive skeletons belonged to whites than to blacks. This trait, however, had no survival value and, thus, had no bearing on biological fitness.

More than 5500 medical and dental students owe their knowledge of anatomy to Dr. Cobb. One student later became chief of surgery at Howard University Hospital.

"Leffall was his name," remembers Dr. Cobb. "He was one of my best students. I had a little custom in my anatomy classes that I called 'bust out.' I'd say who's ready for 'bust out' today. A student would say, 'Come on, doctor, try me.' Then I would try to stump him with questions on material being covered in the classes. At some point, the student might be stumped—*bust out*. He would say 'I'll be ready for you next time.' But Leffall—I could never bust him out."

Many years later, when Dr. Cobb had to undergo surgery,

he insisted on having Dr. Leffall as his surgeon. Leffall brought in a consultant and began to draw lines on Dr. Cobb's abdomen. "Never mind all those lines," said Dr. Cobb. "I want a diagonal incision, one that won't cut through too many nerves and won't show above my bathing trunks. And I want the fine hand of the master on this one. I want you to do everything. The only thing I want your assistant to do is hold the retractors (clamps that hold incision open)."

"Remember I'm the doctor here," said Dr. Leffall with a smile. "You stick to those cadavers."

Later Leffall came into Dr. Cobb's room and said that he was planning to do a diagonal incision.

Anatomy was not Montague Cobb's sole concern. He gave much attention to the problem of racial prejudice which plagued American black people. Cobb felt that white prejudice against black people depended on the myth that black people were a biologically inferior race.

Cobb attacked this myth by summoning all his knowledge of anatomy. He attacked with the facts.

In the 1930's black athletes were breaking most of the records at certain track events, especially the short dash and the broad jump. As a result, the myth arose that black runners were good on the track because of some anatomical features which only black people had. One myth was that the heel bone of blacks was longer than that of whites thus giving black athletes stronger feet.

Dr. Cobb exploded that myth in an article he wrote for the *Journal of Health and Physical Education*. Entitled "Race and Runners", the article pointed out that "There is not a single physical characteristic which all the Negro stars in question have in common which would definitely identify them as Negroes." As proof he compared the physical measurements of some of the famous white and black athletes of the day.

In 1938, when another doctor contended that "a split cartilage in the nose is a reliable test of Negro blood," Dr. Cobb wrote in *The Crisis*, published by the National Association for the Advancement of Colored People, that "available anatomical knowledge indicates quite clearly that no cartilage is known to split in any human nose."

In 1941, addressing a black medical society at Tuskegee, Alabama, Dr. Cobb urged the physicians to mount an all-out attack on the myth of biological inferiority. How must this be done? "Work, sweat and tears," was Dr. Cobb's answer. Black doctors must educate themselves and convince others. He named several books which would give them the facts about the biology of the black person. Only by arming themselves with the facts could they defeat the myths. Such facts had to be made available to government officials who made the laws. Black people had to be made aware of the facts so that their will to achieve would be stimulated.

Gradually, as he gave speeches and wrote articles, the anatomist also became a writer and a crusader for better medical care for black people. Since 1949, he has served as the editor of the *Journal of the National Medical Association*, published by the medical society organized by black doctors in 1895. As the JNMA editor, Dr. Cobb has written hundreds of articles, including over 200 biographies of black healers.

In pamphlets, articles and statements before the United States Congress, Dr. Cobb campaigned for better medical care for black people. He founded and headed the Imhotep National Conference on Hospital Integration, an organization dedicated to removing the color bars in hospitals. He led the fight which eventually resulted in the admission of black physicians to the staff of a Washington hospital. In the course of his career, he has been named to more than sixty scientific boards, advisory and medical activist organizations.

As he has grown older, the honors have come—medals, testimonial dinners, honorary degrees, libraries named after him.

But perhaps the greatest honor is the esteem with which he is held by students, friends and neighbors. Take for example, the young black pharmacist who came to his home on a sunny spring day. Her father was painting Dr. Cobb's house. The father had been urging his daughter to get her Ph.D. in pharmacy. But the daughter wasn't sure. She asked Dr. Cobb for advice. "What do I do with a Ph.D. in pharmacy?" she asked.

Dr. Cobb's advice was both wise and anatomical. "Education should be a pleasure," he said. "Say to yourself 'Do I really want to do this?' Don't be uptight. Listen to Mozart. He's very relaxing. And here's an exercise that will tell you when you're uptight."

Dr. Cobb placed two strips of scotch tape across the woman's forehead. Then he said, "Now when you feel that tape pull you'll know those forehead muscles are tightening up and that'll tell you you're uptight inside.

"Think about it for a while, and if you decide you want to go back to school, come back and we'll make out a program for you."

Anatomy, philosophy, a little music appreciation and some good advice—all these Dr. Cobb had dispersed in just ten minutes.

ARTHUR C. LOGAN

1909–1973

A Harlem Community Doctor

Dr. Arthur C. Logan was a lot of things to a lot of people. If you were a poor and sick old black woman living five flights up in a run-down slum tenement in New York's black community, and you called Arthur Logan at three in the morning, he would come.

When the Rev. Dr. Martin Luther King, Jr. was feeling down and in trouble, Arthur Logan was there. He was one of the few people who could be a pastor to Dr. King.

When "Duke" Ellington, the great black jazz musician, lay sick in a Russian hospital, he telephoned Arthur Logan in New York and asked him to come to his bedside. So Arthur Logan traveled to Russia to be with his ailing patient.

During the Poor People's March on Washington in 1967, Arthur Logan put together a medical team to treat demonstrators camped out in tents.

And when blacks in Harlem picketed at school construction sites to protest the lack of black workers, Dr. Arthur Logan was there in line with the people of his community.

His name was practically a household word in Harlem, New York. Shortly after his death, an old New York hospital was renamed The Arthur C. Logan Memorial Hospital.

"He was my doctor," said 80-year-old Frances Grant sitting in the living room of her St. Nicholas Avenue apartment in New York's Harlem. "Handsome, with shaggy white hair and piercing blue eyes—he was so warm to everybody. Wise in the ways of medicine, wise in the ways of surgery, he treated *people*. He knew enough about each of his patients so that he could always put them at ease. And he could meet 'kings and cats' with no difference," said Miss Grant, as she talked about her doctor and friend.

"The most important thing about Arthur was that he was human. People could call him at any time of day, and he always took time to talk to them. I remember kidding him once when he was examining me in his office. He was taking my blood pressure with one hand and answering the phone with the other. I said, 'now don't get my blood pressure mixed up with somebody's telephone number.' "

Sitting in his office at West 139th Street not far from Miss Grant's apartment, Dr. George Cannon, a longtime friend and associate of Dr. Logan, said, "Well, this is what I said in my tribute at Arthur's funeral in November 1973 . . . *It has been my good fortune and an enrichment of my life to have known Arthur Courtney Logan since his childhood days when he played on West 130th Street and was a student at Ethical Culture School. Our friendship and our professional lives have been intertwined ever since. From the very beginning, in the 1930's when we both opened offices to practice our profession, he showed great interest in the community. When Mayor La Guardia started the Health Insurance Plan . . . he was among the handful who saw the need for a type of medical care that those with a limited income could afford . . . in any program involving community health, right up to the planned creation of a future Knickerbocker Hospital Medical Center, you would always find Arthur Logan giving advice, participating in, if not leading, discussions, and above all, knowledgeable about the subject, its current status in the city or state scheme of things, as well as its local importance . . . But Arthur was more than an organization man. The practice of medicine requires more than the scientific knowledge of health and disease in general. Arthur understood the art of practice as well. To him a patient was not a case but an individual . . . He knew his patients as individuals . . . loyalty to his patients was another outstanding trait . . . When required to sit backstage in the wings of a theatre and watch the performance of a sick patient who insisted that the show must go on, Arthur never hesitated to do the job. He loved his patients and his patients loved him."*

Outside Dr. Cannon's office at the intersection of West 139th Street and 7th Avenue an ambulance, with siren screeching, speeds up the Avenue. On its side, painted in gold letters, is its destination—The Arthur C. Logan Memorial Hospital. It is on its way to Convent Avenue and West 130th Street in West Harlem. Renamed for Dr. Logan in 1974, this private hospital had been known as Knickerbocker Hospital since 1856.

During the last five years of his life, planning for a new Knickerbocker Hospital consumed much of Dr. Logan's time and energy. His goal was the creation of a community health park to replace both the 108-year-old private Knickerbocker Hospital and Sydenham Hospital run by the City of New York. Both were old, run-down and inadequate to meet the health needs of West Harlem, an area populated by nearly 30,000 people.

"Poor people just can't purchase the kind of health care they need and are entitled to," Dr. Logan would say. "The community needs this health center badly. It'll upgrade health services tremendously. It's a community of poor people—a polyglot community with a black and Puerto Rican majority, with a white element mixed in."

The new health park was to cover a six-block area. It was to include a 500 bed, general teaching hospital, a 200 bed nursing home, a 75 bed self-care unit, a mental health center, a medical office building for 40 doctors, a community recreation-social center and over 1,000 low and middle income housing units.

Dr. Logan was the driving force behind this project put together by people in the community. "My role," he would say, "is just relating the two hospitals to each other, Knickerbocker and Sydenham."

At 60 years of age, Dr. Logan was a prominent surgeon as well as a general physician. He had spent most of his professional life working in projects connected with the Harlem community. He was a staff surgeon at the city-run Sydenham Hospital. He still found time for shuttling back and forth between planning sessions for the health center and meeting with high-ranking health and government officials, businessmen, bankers and politicians. He would attend night meetings until well after midnight and still be in the operating room to perform surgery on a patient at seven o'clock in the morning.

Meetings and talks that were not finished during the day would go on at his home late into the night. "Well drop by my house tonight and we'll continue," he would tell people. And often they would arrive at this West 88th Street home before he did and have to wait for him. His home was a whirlwind of activity for anyone who wanted to could come there for help or advice, or to a party to raise money for some educational or social cause for the improvement of conditions for black people or white-black relations in New York.

His day would start around 6 A.M. He cooked himself a big breakfast of eggs, bacon, potatoes, onions, and a pot of coffee to eat while he read the *New York Times*. He would be in the operating room by 7:30 ready to operate. Office hours followed surgery and hospital rounds. Patients came to the office during evening hours too. At home he was always busy. If he wasn't spending time with his son who would stay up until his father came home, Dr. Logan would be reading the latest medical journal or surgical text. Often he'd fall asleep with a journal in his hands. He usually only slept four or five hours a night.

Although New York City was Arthur Logan's home, his roots were in the deep south—Tuskegee, Alabama. His father, Warren Logan, was the first treasurer of the famed Tuskegee Institute under Booker T. Washington in 1882. At age nine, Arthur Logan went to live with an older sister in New York. This move was perhaps the beginning that shaped his approach to life and his career in medicine.

His older sister, Ruth, was already a doctor when Arthur joined her. Her husband, Arthur's brother-in-law, was Dr. E.P. Roberts, the second black doctor to practice medicine in New York City. He was also the first black doctor to serve on the Board of Health of New York City. In 1910 Dr. Roberts had been one of the founders of the National Urban League. So Arthur Logan found himself growing up in a medical atmosphere and being raised by two people involved in social and civic affairs in the early Harlem community.

From the Ethical Culture School in New York, Logan entered Williams College in western Massachusetts in 1926. Williams was a lonely place for Arthur and the six other black students. It was his first exposure to racial prejudice by whites, but the bonds between Arthur and the six other black students were strong, and they supported each other. In his junior year,

Arthur Logan was awarded a Phi Beta Kappa key for excellent performance in his studies.

In 1930, Arthur Logan was in the freshman class at Columbia University's College of Physicians and Surgeons in New York. Four years later he graduated with his M.D. degree, and from 1934 to 1936 he did his internship at Harlem Hospital.

"These were the real depression days," Logan once said. "The days of the first widespread, hardcore poverty among black people in New York City, and the days of a huge migration of black people from the rural south." The health problems of poor black people in Harlem were to become the problems that shaped his life as a doctor.

In 1936 his sister Ruth and her husband, E.P. Roberts, were practicing medicine from a basement office on West 130th Street in the center of Harlem. Upon finishing his training at Harlem Hospital, Logan moved in with them to begin his medical career. He worked from West 130th Street for six years before opening up his own office.

Arthur Logan was a noted surgeon at Harlem Hospital from 1936 to 1962. He had been trained in surgery by Dr. Louis T. Wright.

In 1969 when the surgical wing of the new Harlem Hospital Center was named in honor of Dr. Wright, Arthur Logan was one of those who paid tribute to Dr. Wright at ceremonies in the hospital auditorium. Logan said in his tribute—"I have been blessed not once, but three times in knowledge of and proud friendship with Edward Kennedy Ellington, known as Duke, with Martin Luther King, Jr., and with the man whom we honor, although inadequately, today—Louis Tompkins

Wright." Dr. Wright had been an important person in the development of Arthur Logan as a surgeon.

Dr. Logan was happy at Harlem Hospital, but was attracted to Sydenham Hospital through his work with private patients. He was always concerned with the needs of the total community, and when Harlem Hospital joined with Columbia's School of Physicians and Surgeons, Logan felt the medical school would benefit more than the people of Harlem. So, he resigned from the Harlem Hospital in 1962 and joined Sydenham.

Arthur Logan had an incredible number of friends from all walks of life. His friendship with the famed musician Duke Ellington was perhaps best known. Dr. Logan had gone around the corner and around the globe many times just to care for Ellington. "Duke wouldn't cross the street without first asking Arthur," said Logan's sister, Dr. Myra Logan.

Duke Ellington's band was playing at the Cotton Club in New York in 1947. His lead saxophonist suffered a severe asthma attack before performance time, and Ellington asked his road manager to find a doctor quickly. Dr. Logan was called to the Cotton Club, where he treated Ellington's ailing band member with an injection of adrenalin. In a few minutes the sax player was breathing easily and was ready for the show.

Two days later Ellington himself was feeling sick, and he remembered meeting Arthur Logan. He asked his road manager to make an appointment with Dr. Logan, and this was the beginning of the Logan-Ellington friendship. Over the years Dr. Logan attended Ellington in such far-away places as Russia, Pakistan and India. Ellington would call his doctor in New York from all parts of the world when he didn't feel the way he felt he should. Dr. Logan was Duke Ellington's doctor for 37 years.

Dr. Logan loved to entertain at his home in New York City and he would do the cooking—soul food, roasts, steaks; at lunch a special meat or fish. There were always more than good times, good music and good food.

There were also serious conversations with Dr. Martin Luther King, Jackie Robinson, baseball's first black player, and other leaders of New York City—black and white. If you wanted to raise money to fight drug traffic in Harlem, or help make Charles Evers the first black mayor in Mississippi, or send some black South African kid to college, Logan's doors were always open to let you speak for any cause that would bring a better life for black and poor people in New York or anywhere in the country. When Dr. Logan passed away, Mayor Lindsay called Logan "a civic leader of extraordinary intelligence and devotion, who somehow found the time and energy to express the widest range of social concerns while carrying the full load of medical practice and involvement in the medical community."

In his home there was a wall he called Martin's Wall. On it hung photographs of Martin Luther King, Jr. taken in Logan's home and on his various travels around the world. The civil rights leader was a close friend of the Logans. It was Logan's wife Marian who introduced her husband to Rev. Dr. King. She had been an activist supporter and fund-raiser for the black student sit-ins of the early 1960's. King and his doctor away from home often debated civil rights tactics when King visited the Logan home.

Just as Arthur Logan had an incredible number of friends,

he worked for an incredible number of social and civic causes. He volunteered his time, energy and talents to city, state and national groups. He was an active member in the NAACP Legal Aid and Defense Fund, the Harlem Urban Development Corporation, the National Urban League, the Harlem Youth Opportunities Unlimited (HARYOU), the National Medical Association, the Southern Christian Leadership Conference, the Council Against Poverty and United Neighborhood Houses—to name just a few. "And he was an active member," said Dr. Kenneth Clark, HARYOU's first board chairman. "He wasn't just a name on our Board list—he really cared about our work to get jobs and education for black youth. He gave the organization the kind of personal attention he would give a patient."

His deep concern for the health care of people with little income was always present. In 1948 when Mayor Wagner okayed a health insurance plan for New York City, Dr. Logan was one of the chief organizers of the Upper Manhattan Medical Group—a team of doctors who provided pre-paid, low cost medical care for the poor. Dr. Logan served as Chief of Surgery for this health clinic.

What was one of the most significant things about Dr. Arthur Logan? "He was an inspiration to people, particularly young people," said his wife, Marian Logan. "He proved that a black man, and particularly a black man who looked so white, could not only survive, but could become a meaningful, effective member of the black community. He was able to inspire other black youngsters to become not only doctors but to get a good educational background so they could become the best in whatever field they entered. He warned those who wanted to be doctors that medicine was hard work.''

Arthur Logan dedicated the last years of his life to promoting financial and moral support for a Manhattanville Health Center that was to replace Knickerbocker and Sydenham Hospitals. Tremendous hurdles lay in the way of this project— getting money to plan and build, and enough land in the right place near the old Knickerbocker. If housing had to be torn down to make room for the new health center, then new housing had to be built before the new hospital for those whose homes would be taken. Logan worked on the problems day and night.

There was a city bus depot just a block away from the Knickerbocker, at Amsterdam and West 129th Street. If the huge garage were moved to another site, this land could be used for the new health center. Dr. Logan kept his eye on this location for several years, and in late November, 1973, he learned that the bus depot could be relocated.

A possible new site for the bus terminal was 12th Avenue between 133rd and 134th Streets. Arthur Logan went alone to view the site on a late November day in 1973. Tragically, it was to be his last day. He fell to his death from a point on the Henry Hudson Parkway, overlooking the site that perhaps would have helped to make his health center a reality.

"It may take ten years to complete the Manhattanville Health Center," Dr. Logan said in 1970.

The project to which Arthur Logan dedicated himself is still not a reality today, but the planning goes on, and when the center is finished, Dr. Arthur C. Logan will be remembered.

DANIEL A. COLLINS

1916–

Dentist, Scientist

Dan Collins was born in Darlington, South Carolina, into a world of work. His mother taught school and ran a small store. His father had his own heavy equipment company. The company moved houses, timber, anything that was heavy and needed moving.

When he was old enough, Dan learned about work. He worked as a gardener. He sold newspapers. He worked for a butcher, cleaning and selling fish. He still remembers the picture of the pony he kept on the mantle. Sell enough talcum powder and you had a chance to win the pony. Dan's reward was his own spending money.

But his parents' labors produced an even more important reward for Dan—a good and loving home. It was a good home to grow up in, a place where a young person could feel safe and secure. Looking back from adulthood, Dan Collins would often say that it was there in that home that he learned to use the best that was in him.

For Dan Collins there has been a lot of "best." He grew up to be dentist, research scientist, health educator, writer, editor and corporate executive.

But had Dan Collins, the teenager, been able to look into the future and see Dan Collins, the adult, he might have been quite surprised. For there would be many a twist and turn to his life.

Every class has a fat kid. At Mayo High School in Darlington, Dan Collins was the class fatty. At 236 pounds he was nearly as wide as he was tall. His classmates teased him. Girls ignored him. And what was worse, Dan agreed with them. Fat was not nice. All of this added up to an unhappy Dan Collins. Dan showed his unhappiness by throwing spitballs and talking in class. He studied only enough to get by on. His family expected him to stay in school and go on to college, and so he stuck it out.

There was one good thing about his size. Dan was a star on the football team. When a teacher gave him a failing grade, Dan thought he deserved better since he was a football star. He thought of a good way to get even with the whole school. He'd turn in his uniform. That'd fix them. They wouldn't win anymore games.

Dan was really getting off on the wrong track. Then he met I. C. Wiley, a math teacher at Mayo High School.

Dan has always had a talent for math. Without studying he often did well in class. Mr. Wiley encouraged Dan to work harder on his math. Dan was soon leading the class. The taste of success spurred him to work harder in his other classes. Dan was beginning to believe in himself. It was an important step for him. By the time he entered Paine College in Augusta, Georgia, Dan Collins had become a good student. He chose chemistry for his major subject.

He did so well in chemistry that he was made a student lab assistant. This meant that he had to be responsible for seeing that all the equipment and chemicals were ready for the students. But he also was given small projects to do, chemicals to analyze. He began to see that there was lots more to know. The first seed was planted in the mind of the future scientist.

But chemistry was not the only thing Dan Collins learned at Paine College. He also learned some important things about people.

Throughout his school years in Darlington, Dan had never had a white teacher. At Paine the faculty was one-half black and one-half white. Later he was to write about this experience in a church magazine. "By the time I entered Paine College as a freshman, I had hardly ever encountered a white person whom I could identify as friendly or who had any concern for me or my kind beyond the immediate business at hand . . . In 1932, had I known about the interracial commitment at Paine College, I might have been too terrified of southern whites to become a part of that freshman class . . . Paine College proved to be an oasis in a desert of poor race relations. It was there that I met intelligent, concerned and dedicated white southerners who . . . accepted my feelings of human equality. It was there that I began to know that white and black people had much more in common and much more to share than not. The black and white teachers . . . helped to strengthen my ailing self image, a great need growing out of the heritage of any southern black male. Even in the early 1930's, on Paine campus I never once was made conscious of my blackness or felt the need to recognize another's whiteness."

Dan Collins completed his studies at Paine College in 1936. He had done so well in college that his professor urged him to go on and study more chemistry in graduate school. But he couldn't see himself as a chemist. He wanted to be a construction engineer, work with his father, and build bridges and highways.

To get a taste of the work after completing his college education, he went to work for his father moving houses. His father worked all over the state of South Carolina on projects that might take weeks to complete. That meant they could not come home each night after a day's work, so Dan's father would rent a house near his job. He'd hire a cook, and the crew would live there until the job was finished. Sometimes they'd get home on weekends. But it was a camp life, and Dan didn't care much for it.

Something had happened while Dan had been away at college which made him change his mind about being a construction engineer. During Dan's high school years, his father had been his own boss. Mr. Collins was the outstanding house mover in the state. But when the state began a big highway construction program, it set up its own house moving division. This meant that Dan's father was forced to work under state officials. People who had no experience at all became his father's bosses because he was black and they were white. It didn't bother the father too much; he was used to it. But it was a blow to the son. Out of his unhappiness and disappointment came the idea to become a physician.

Dan Collins applied to two black medical schools, Howard and Meharry, but there were no openings. However, Meharry, in Nashville, Tennessee, said they had some openings in dentistry. "I'll take it," Dan Collins wrote back.

His grades were excellent at Meharry. Projects with vitamin research increased Dan Collins' interest in research. When he graduated he was offered a chance to study at the Guggenheim Dental Clinic in New York City. There he was trained in dentistry for children. Much research on tooth decay in children was taking place at Guggenheim, and the new Dr. Collins had a small part in that.

Dr. Collins had just finished his year at Guggenheim when he was offered a chance to do post graduate study at the University of California in San Francisco, California. There he could devote full time to research, something he found more and more interesting. He planned to get his master's degree in dentistry and then go back to Meharry and teach. There he would settle down to a career of teaching and research.

At the University of California, Dr. Collins began to study and do research under the guidance of Dr. Hermann Becks. Dr. Becks was a physician and dentist who headed the division of Dental Medicine. The division studied the cause of tooth disease and the prevention of tooth loss.

Dr. Collins was awarded his Masters degree in dentistry in 1944. In the months before he earned his degree, Dr. Collins had been exchanging letters with officials at Meharry about his joining the Meharry faculty. Although Meharry had a black student body, the top administrators and many of the instructors and professors were white. Quite by accident he learned that black instructors were paid less than white instructors of the same rank. "I could not live with that," he remembers. "People may be superior to me because of certain abilities but not because of skin color."

The president of Meharry wrote that, if Dr. Collins came back to his old school, he would have to accept things as they were.

Dr. Collins decided to stay at the University of California. He was appointed an instructor in the College of Dentistry. And he continued working under Dr. Becks. He and Dr. Becks worked with the very famous Herbert M. Evans who headed the Institute of Experimental Biology. Out of Dr. Evans' labs had come much important research.

In the Evans lab the 48 human chromosomes had been discovered. Chromosomes are those tiny threads of protein and nucleic acids that direct inheritance from within the cell. There in the Evans lab it had been discovered that vitamin E is essential for the reproduction of mammals. Important research was being done in Dr. Evans' lab on how chemicals called hormones direct many vital activities of the body. Dr. Dan Collins felt truly honored and fortunate to be working here.

Much of Dr. Evans' hormone research was done in the following manner. The gland known to produce the hormone to be studied was removed from the rat. Then different research teams studied the effects of the hormone deficiency on the different parts of the body. Some teams looked at the long bones; others studied the kidneys, heart, lungs and other organs. Dr. Collins was on the team that studied the head, face, jaw and teeth.

In one project, Dr. Collins studied the effect of the lack of certain hormones on the temporomandibular joint, or the jaw joint. The proper functioning of this joint is crucial to the health of the teeth. A diseased or injured jaw joint can cause the teeth to grind abnormally against each other, producing pain and damaged teeth.

So that he would know what to look for, Dr. Collins studied the jaw joints of normal rats of different ages ranging from 5 days to 4 months. He used two techniques to make his studies—X rays and microscopic. The mice were first killed, then the X rays made. Next very thin slices of the jaw joint were made and placed on slides. These slides were then examined microscopically.

As he studied the jaw joint in older and older normal rats, a pattern of growth and development of the joint began to emerge. In the youngest rats, the rounded end of the jawbone was made up of cartilage. Gradually as the rat grew older, more and more of the cartilage was replaced with bone cells, until only the very outer part of the bone end remained cartilaginous. As more and more cartilage was replaced by bone, the joint was less able to withstand the stress of disease and injury.

Next Dr. Collins studied month-old rats who had had their pituitary gland removed by surgery. The pituitary located at the base of the brain is sometimes called the master gland. The pituitary produces many hormones which regulate vital processes. One hormone produced by the pituitary is called growth hormone. This hormone is known to regulate the growth and development of many bones. But no one knew much about the effect of growth hormone on the growth of the jawbone. By studying rats who lacked a pituitary gland, Dr. Collins could find out what the lack of growth hormone might do to the jaw joint.

Dr. Collins studied the jaw joint of the rat without pituitaries using the same procedure as before. Studies were made on rats from 4 days to 5 months after their surgery. What Dr. Collins saw was a very rapid aging of the jaw joint. The jaw joints of those rats who had gone without growth hormone for 28 days had rapidly progressed to the final stage of aging found in much older normal rats.

The research seemed to show that growth hormone did affect the jaw joint and hence dental health. But Dr. Collins needed more proof. This led to the third stage of the experiment.

To prove his theory, Dr. Collins injected the hormone into another group of rats who had had their pituitaries removed.

Like the other group without pituitaries, the jaw bones of these rats were severely aged.

The growth hormone had a dramatic effect on the ends of the aging jawbones. The bone ends began to thicken with cartilage. After 39 days of injections, the bones had been restored to a healthy youthful state.

This experiment with growth hormone injections seemed to prove that the pituitary had a role in dental health. And another bit of knowledge was now available to the dentist trying to diagnose a puzzling case. Now a study of pituitary function became a diagnostic tool for the dentist.

What effect did the pituitary have on the teeth? Studies of rats without pituitaries revealed the answer. The structure of the tooth began to break down. The pulp, the inner core containing the blood circulation system of the tooth, began to shrink. Holes appeared in the hard outer enamel layer. The tooth became misshaped.

This was for Dr. Collins the high point of his research. The discovery that removing a gland could actually control the growth of a tooth was very exciting to him. He had found an important control of dental health.

A medical fad in the 1940's led Dr. Collins into his next research project. The fad was vitamin D. Vitamin D was supposed to cure everything from colds to tuberculosis to rashes. People were flocking to the drugstore where they could buy big bottles of capsules without a prescription.

University of California nutritionist Dr. Agnes Morgan asked Dr. Collins to study the physical effects of huge vitamin D doses. Testing large doses on dogs revealed the great hazard of large vitamin doses. Dr. Collins found that vitamin

D actually made the calcium in the bones move into the bloodstream. Then, when the vitamin D dosage was stopped, the calcium spilled out of the blood into the tissues. The calcium clogged the blood vessels in vital organs like the kidneys and lungs. Tissue deprived of life-giving blood circulation died. The calcium clogged the blood circulation within the pulp of the tooth. The tooth became distorted and weak.

Other scientists were finding that the vitamin was particularly harmful to children. They found that too much vitamin D could produce deformed faces, mental illness and heart trouble.

When the scientific reports of Dr. Collins and the other scientists were released, the action of the government was swift. The Food and Drug Administration (FDA) issued orders that the amount of vitamin D added to milk be reduced. The FDA also ruled that only regulated amounts of vitamin D could be sold without a prescription.

In addition to his research, Dr. Collins also treated patients in his dental office. One case history he has always saved. It tells the story of two small boys afflicted with an inherited disorder called ectodermal dysplasia. Something had gone wrong with their development as tiny unborn babies. As a result they were born with many problems. They had only wispy eyebrows and hair. The hair problem plus very high foreheads made them a little strange looking. Their classmates made their lives miserable, and the boys were doing poorly in school.

The boys had no sweat glands. The evaporation of perspiration cools the normal person during hot weather. Deprived of a natural cooling system, the boys developed high fevers and convulsions during hot weather.

Moving from the hot climate of Fresno, California, to cooler San Francisco helped the sweat gland problem. When the boys walked into Dr. Collins' office they were hoping for a solution to another problem. They wanted teeth. One boy had only two teeth. The other had six stubby teeth.

Dr. Collins examined their mouths. Then he made models of their mouths and had upper and lower dentures made for the boys.

Photos in the boys' case history envelope show the result. The *before* photo shows two solemn-eyed boys. One has the sunken mouth of a person with no teeth. The *after* photo shows two smiling, apparently normal boys.

"When I put in their teeth, their eyes lit up, and they gave me a big hug," says Dr. Collins. "That was the biggest paycheck I ever got."

Teeth made a big difference in the lives of the boys. Now they could eat and speak better. They began to do better in school. One brother became an Eagle Scout. Fitting the boys with teeth was a simple solution to a serious problem.

But the diagnosis and treatment of patients is not always so simple for a dentist. One serious problem is finding the reason for strange pains of the jaws, teeth and face. In fact, the problem of pain had so intrigued Dr. Collins that he went to the medical library and read all the research papers he could find on the subject. He found that there was a great deal of knowledge, much of it not taught to dental students. Pain is the result of the activation of a nerve cell. The message travels along the nervous system to the brain, and the person feels the pain. Dr. Collins found that several different problems can activate the pain impulse. Often the problems narrowed down to malfunctioning blood vessels and muscles, as well as the irritation and inflammation of the teeth and jaw bone.

To help patients with strange pains, Dr. Collins and another dentist organized the Consultative Oral and Facial Pain Service at the University of California Dental School. Patients who came to the service were first asked many questions about how the pain felt, when it happened, what seemed to bring it on, and what seemed to help it. X rays and a physical examination of the jaw, the mouth and the neck were done.

One woman had damaged her jaw joint by biting a carrot. This produced pain on the left side of her face. She was told to be careful not to open her mouth too wide. Worry that she might have cancer added to her problems. She was told that she did not have cancer. Relief from worry and cautious opening of the mouth eventually made the pain go away.

Another woman was found to be grinding her teeth in her sleep. This irritated the muscles of the jaw and neck and produced the pain. She was given a special splint to wear over the lower teeth at night. This prevented her unconscious tooth grinding. Within four days she began to get relief.

But not all people who brought their pain to the Service were so successfully treated. One man came in with such severe facial pain that he could not even bear to wash his face. One of Dr. Collins associates was able to stop the pain by injecting alcohol in the nerve to stop the pain impulse. But they were never able to find the cause of the pain.

Dr. Collins' work at the University of California was interrupted in 1956 by a call into the army. After basic training, he was assigned to the Armed Forces Institute of Pathology at the Walter Reed Hospital in Washington, D. C.

The Dental Division of the Armed Forces Institute of Pathology was under the command of Colonel Joseph Barnier. "Set me up a research program," were the orders the colonel gave to Dr. Collins. The first project Dr. Collins set up involved testing the effects of a new way of grinding teeth that had just been developed. The new method, called high speed instrumentation, was fast and not as uncomfortable as the old method of grinding. But some dentists were concerned that the new technique might harm the delicate nerves within the tooth. Dr. Collins and other members of the staff set up an experiment with dogs in which the effect of high speed instrumentation on nerves could be tested.

Dr. Collins also began to study the cancers that might affect dental health. He was also continuing his pain research. As a top staff member, he had the chance to work with many other pathologists. Pathologists study the cause and the effect of disease.

Pathology taught him the different kinds of things that can happen to a nerve. He learned that cut nerves can form tiny swellings on the cut end, called a neuroma. The neuroma can trigger pain. It is this phenomenon which produces the so-called "phantom pain," pain which a person feels in an amputated arm or leg. And neuromas on cut nerves in the mouth could also produce strange, difficult-to-diagnose pain.

By 1958, Dr. Collins had finished his army service. He headed back to California full of ideas for research he would like to continue. The University of California had modern laboratories. It was an ideal place to do research in dentistry.

But first, Dr. Collins thought he had earned a promotion to a permanent position on the staff. As an associate professor, he could study his own research ideas. He would have more people and more labs in which to study those ideas. He had taught on the University of California dental faculty for 16 years. He had 25 pieces of published research to his credit, received honors and awards for his research. He had a graduate degree, a diploma of the oral pathology board, in addition to his dental degree. And he had written chapters for textbooks. He felt well qualified to be an associate professor.

But still he wasn't sure how the University would respond to his promotion request. A close friend of his had pushed for promotion a year earlier. He, too, was well qualified. He was Jewish. And no Jew or oriental or black had ever been appointed to the rank of associate professor on the dental faculty. The friend did not make it. Dr. Collins' promotion was also turned down.

It was a very low point for him. Looking around, he could see that he was as well qualified as any of the other associate professors in the Dental School. The injustice of it hurt deeply. His university career had come to a dead end. He saw all his research in the past coming to an end. Would anyone do more research to learn more about his discoveries? And what about the new ideas he wanted to try? What would happen to them?

Dr. Collins left his job on the dental faculty and went into the full-time practice of dentistry.

His patients reaped the rewards of those many years of research. One woman was especially fortunate to have brought her problem to Dr. Collins. For six months, she had been troubled with pain in the upper left face. She had been to many dentists and physicians. But they had done little for her except give her prescriptions for pain killers.

Dr. Collins looked into the woman's mouth and almost at once pinpointed the problem. There was a large painful, swollen area in the left side of the roof of her mouth. It looked like cancer of the maxillary sinus. Lab tests confirmed it. Treatment meant cutting out part of the roof of the mouth. The woman refused to have the disfiguring surgery. "I'm going to travel," she said, "and think."

Six months later, the woman agreed to the surgery. But she had lost precious time. The cancer had grown and the possibility that it had spread to other parts of the body was also greater. But she came through the surgery well. She was fitted with an artificial palate and was soon able to eat and speak.

Whether or not the cancer recurred because of spreading, Dr. Collins was not to know, for after several follow-up checkups, Dr. Collins never saw her again.

After he left the University of California, Dr. Collins began to devote more and more time to community service. He was appointed to many commissions and boards, such as the mayor's committee on youth, the California State Board of Public Health and a presidental appointment to the National Health Resources Advisory Committee. But the appointment that changed his life was the one naming him to the California State Board of Public Education. "Here was a chance to work for all the four million kids in California," he says. He had four sons. He had seen the books they used. And there was something that had always bothered him about the books. Black people were shown as depressed, inferior, non-achieving people. True, Booker T. Washington, George Washington Carver, and Jackie Robinson were in the books. But beyond that there seemed little to admire about the black people in the textbooks. But being on the Public Education Board was a chance to do something about the content of textbooks.

After talking to publishers, the Board learned that publishers could only profitably publish books that people would buy. The Board decided to take a hard look at the kinds of books California would buy. They asked the Department of History of the University of California to study the textbooks used by California students. The study showed that many different kinds of people were unfairly depicted in the books.

The result was that the Board, with the backing of the governor, pushed through a new law. The law said that California would not accept any book which did not include a fair representation of ethnic groups, women, men, labor, management and many other groups.

In one year, publishers changed many books. One publisher wrote a completely new history book which showed the contribution of many different people to history. Despite several attacks on the book, it was eventually accepted in many southern states. From that point on, many publishers began to look to California for guidance on what books the education departments of the states would buy.

In 1968 Dr. Collins wrote his own book entitled *Your Teeth: A handbook of dental care for the whole family*. He also wrote several articles on dentistry for Encyclopedia Americana Science Supplement. And by 1970, he was asked to head a newly established division of a textbook publishing company.

Now he has greatly reduced the time spent in dental practice, and is spending most of his time in publishing. He is full of ideas he wants his readers to understand. He says, "I want the student to learn to love himself. I want him to learn how to make decisions. I want to inform him of the things that will endanger him. I want him to understand that many diseases are determined by lifestyle—rest, food, hygiene, etc. There is no way a doctor can keep up with all the diseases a person can produce for himself. Each person must learn how to prevent disease and how to maintain good health."

But Dr. Collins still looks back wistfully at his decision to leave the University of California and research. "I think," he says, "if things had been different, I would have liked to have spent my entire life in research and teaching."

JANE C. WRIGHT

1919–

Enemy of Cancer

For Jane Wright, the daughter of Dr. Louis Wright, it seemed only natural to study medicine. Her father was a great man; what better thing to do with her life than to follow in his footsteps?

She remembers his influence every step of the way. Once, as a medical student, she was struggling to learn the life cycle of certain worms and other human parasites. Her father amazed her by reciting life cycle after life cycle. As a New York physician, he seldom had contact with parasitic diseases which are common in tropical areas. And yet he remembered those life cycles.

As a young physician in 1949, Dr. Jane Wright received her first medical assignment from her father. She went to work for the Cancer Research Foundation of Harlem Hospital, a cancer study unit organized by her father.

Dr. Wright's weapon against cancer has been chemicals. Because they grow more rapidly than most normal cells, cancer cells are especially sensitive to certain chemicals. Rapid growth means they have more needs than the normal cells of the body, and certain chemicals can interfere with these needs.

In the early 1950's, when Dr. Wright began her campaign against cancer, the idea of fighting cancer with chemicals was still experimental. Cancer chemotherapy had its beginnings on a battlefield in France during World War I. A number of American infantrymen had been gassed by the Germans. In the field hospital, it was discovered that the gas had damaged the bodily system that makes white blood cells. Since the overproduction of white blood cells is the most important feature of blood cancer (leukemia) the gas seemed to be a way to treat leukemia. The gas was mustard gas. By 1946, scientists had developed a liquid called nitrogen mustard which helped leukemia victims when injected into a vein. Later research was to prove nitrogen mustard effective against other cancers.

Nitrogen mustard is an alkylating chemical. This means that it adds chemical groups to certain substances in the cell where such chemicals should not be, thus disrupting cell division and, in turn, growth of the cancer. Dr. Wright began her career as a cancer researcher by studying another chemical called triethylene melamine (TEM), thought also to be an effective alkylating agent against cancer. TEM had been proven effective against leukemia in mice. Dr. Wright decided to try it against certain human leukemias and cancers of the lymphatic system such as Hodgkin's disease. She had the patient take one dose of TEM every day for a week. This was followed by one dose a week for five more weeks. Within two weeks 10 out of 11 victims of Hodgkins disease began to feel better. Their painful swollen glands in the neck shrank. The abdominal pains ceased. For some, TEM halted the disease for five years before they needed more treatment. Further testing showed TEM to be equally effective against four other types of cancer similar to Hodgkins.

But neither nitrogen mustard nor TEM were effective against severe leukemia or many other kinds of cancer. Dr. Wright decided to test a new group of anti-cancer chemicals called antimetabolites. Such chemicals block the production of important chemicals in the cancer cell's nucleus.

Checking through the wards of Harlem Hospital, Dr. Wright selected 93 cancer patients whom surgery and radiation had failed to help. She started the patients on doses of different antimetabolites. Of the 93 cases, 54 showed improvement of some kind. Although they had been helped, for a while, most of the patients later died of cancer, but chemicals had given them more time.

There seemed to be a bright promise to chemotherapy. Dr. Wright accepted a new job at New York University Medical Center where she began to explore that promise.

Now Dr. Wright began looking for ways to perfect the use of chemicals. She knew that there were at least 20 or 30 anti-cancer chemicals. But which ones worked best for which cancers? Shouldn't there be a better way to determine that than just by giving a lot of patients doses of different chemicals and then watching for the disappearance of the cancer?

Then she hit on an idea. Why not let the cancer cells, themselves, tell the story. She would study changes in the cancer cells as the chemical did its work. She would then have a test tube method of predicting the effect of different drugs on the more than 100 known types of cancers.

Basically the experiment would work like this. A tiny bit of the patient's tumor would be removed at surgery and placed in a flask of protein-rich fluid. By carefully regulating the temperature and the chemicals in the flask, Dr. Wright would grow the tumor cells in what is called a tissue culture. Then the chemical to be tested would be added to the flask of cells. At the same time, the patient would be started on doses of the same chemical. Microscopic views of the cells in the flasks would be compared with the condition of the patient. This meant that cell changes could be compared with cancer changes. Thus, Dr. Wright would get a microscopic view of what was happening to the cancer.

For example, one patient with Hodgkin's Disease had painfully swollen lymph nodes in his neck. A tiny bit of one of those nodes was removed and grown in a tissue culture. TEM, the alkylating chemical, was added to the tissue culture. At the same time the man was started on doses of TEM. After several weeks of TEM therapy, the nodes in the man's neck began to shrink. A check of the cells in the tissue culture showed wholesale destruction of the cells. Nucleii were broken and discolored. Cytoplasm had all but disappeared.

Now she had a new tool for studying the chemotherapy of cancer. Once she knew the kind of cell changes to look for in each kind of tumor, Dr. Wright could then use tissue culture of cancer cells to determine the best chemical to use on a certain cancer. In the case of Hodgkins, for example, cell destruction seemed to be the thing to look for when testing an anti-cancer chemical.

She also found that tissue culture was an excellent way to find out exactly how a new chemical stopped the cancer. When a new anti-cancer chemical made from the periwinkle plant became available, Dr. Wright tested it in tissue culture. Studying the cancer cells, after they had been exposed to the chemical for 96 hours, she discovered that the cytoplasm had shrunk, and the nucleus had split into several parts. And most of the cells had simply stopped in an early stage of division. Dr. Wright's theory was that the new chemical interfered with cell division and that it did so by blocking the role of the cell's cytoplasm in cell division.

From that experiment she went on to laboratory testing of other cancers and other chemicals. Now when a new cancer victim was admitted to the hospital, Dr. Wright could consult her charts produced through research to find the best chemical to give the patient. Just to be sure, she would check tissue culture of the patient's cancer cells with the chemical.

Now Dr. Wright turned her attention to better ways of getting the chemical to the cancer cells. From her work with tissue culture, she had decided that giving the chemical by mouth or injection was not always the most effective way of delivering the chemical to the cancer cells deep inside the body, for the chemical might have to travel quite a distance through many parts of the body before it reached the cancerous area. By then some of the chemical might have been picked up by other parts of the body.

Other scientists had developed a technique called perfusion. This meant injecting the chemical into the major blood vessel supplying the cancer. It was often used as a kind of mopping-up operation of stray cancer cells following the surgical removal of a tumor. But now Dr. Wright could see other uses for perfusion. Perfusion could be a simple way to deliver the chemical directly to the tumor. And there were other advantages, too. Most chemicals produced side effects in patients since they attacked any cell in rapid growth. Typical side effects were nausea and lowering of resistance to infection. But if the chemical could be routed directly to the tumor, side effects could certainly be reduced if not avoided altogether.

Also the perfusion technique seemed an excellent way of treating patients who had a cancer that could not be removed by surgeons because of its location or extensive spread. And perfusion could be the answer for patients facing the amputation of a cancerous limb.

Dr. Wright began a test of perfusion as a way of giving

chemotherapy to cancer patients. She tested 52 patients, with cancers of the head, neck, legs, ovary and other areas. The perfusion technique involved locating the major artery and vein serving the cancerous area. Using a special needle, the artery and vein were connected. Tourniquets were used to prevent the chemical from leaking out of the circulatory detour into the rest of the body. Then the chemical was pumped into the needle connecting the two blood vessels.

Dr. Wright found that this technique seemed to work best on tumors of the head, limbs and pelvis. Studying some of the cancers after perfusion, she noted that first the tumor grew dark and dry. Then it started to break up and shrink. Out of the 52 patients she studied, 32 were helped by the procedure. But no tumor disappeared completely.

It has been a long road—this chemical search for a cure for cancer—and still no cure has been found. But Dr. Wright has seen cancer slowed by chemicals. One success she is very proud of is her battle against a fatal form of skin cancer—a disease which surgery and radiation cannot help. The disease often produces horrible disfigurement of the person's face. One man treated by Dr. Wright had the disease over his entire body, except for his hands, feet and scalp. Huge bluish red lumps twisted his face out of shape. But after 30 days of treatment with chemicals, his face was completely clear with only a few whitish scars where the lumps had been. His disease flared up several times. But each time it was stopped by chemotherapy.

The world of test tubes and hospital beds is not the only place where Dr. Wright has waged a battle against cancer. In 1963 she was asked to serve on the President's Commission on Heart Disease, Cancer, and Stroke. After many meetings the commission came to the conclusion that better use needed to be made of medical research. The commission recommended that disease centers be located in different parts of the country. In those centers all that is known about diagnosing and treating the diseases would be put into action.

Dr. Wright has received many awards honoring her work in cancer chemotherapy. She often uses such occasions to urge people to be on the alert for the symptoms of cancer and to seek prompt treatment.

On April 10, 1975, she received the "Finer Womanhood Award" during a celebration of International Year of Women at Clark College in Atlanta, Georgia. The award was given by the Black Women's International Conference on Priorities and Directives.

This was part of Dr. Wright's speech:

"Since my major interest in medicine through the years has been with cancer, I thought that I would share with you some of the shocking facts about this disease, since they are very much with us.

"Cancer is the second leading cause of death in the United States today. Only accidents take a greater toll.

"In the 1970's, it is estimated that there will be 3.5 million cancer deaths, and more than 10 million under care for cancer. These figures indicate the enormous problem presented by this disease in the present state of medical knowledge.

"At the turn of the century, in the early 1900's, there was little hope of any cure for cancer patients. With the knowledge we have today, one third of the patients who develop cancer will be cured for five or more years. There are now 1.5 million people in this country living and cured of cancer. But if all of the knowledge we have accumulated could be broadly applied to every man, woman, and child in the United States, approximately 50 percent of the people who develop cancer could be cured. Thus our immediate goal for the control of cancer is the annual saving of the lives of half of those who develop cancer. This can be done by early diagnosis and prompt treatment. The future goal of complete cancer control is only possible through research.''

And what kind of research will provide the cure for cancer? Dr. Wright thinks the problem should be attacked from all directions. The virologist should work on identifying the viruses that cause cancer. The surgeon should continue to look for better ways to remove cancer. Radiation and chemotherapy research should continue. She thinks chemotherapy will be the approach that wins the race.

"I've seen chemicals do enough," she says. "For the future we need newer and better chemicals."

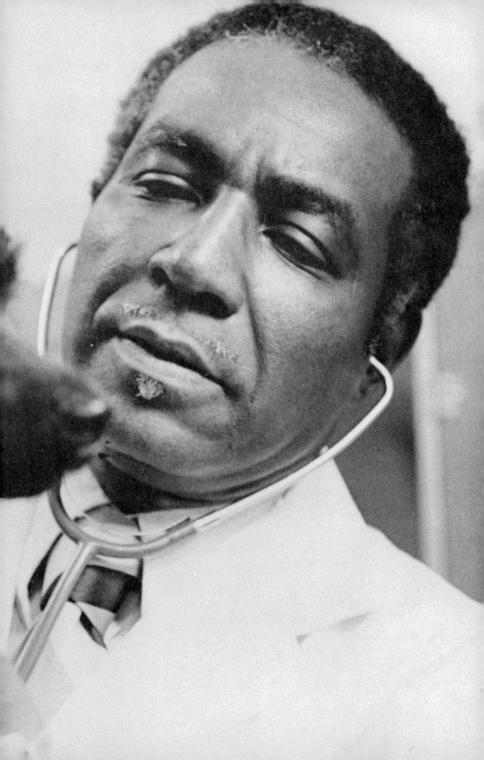

EUGENE W. ADAMS

1920–

Caring For Animals

"There is really little difference between animal medicine and human medicine. Diseases in animals and humans are very similar. When an animal has pneumonia or cancer, the symptoms are the same as in man. And so are the changes in body organs and tissues. Infections in dogs and man are the same kind of problem.

"While veterinary or animal medicine is concerned with the disease and health of animals, it plays an important role in human health because we live so close to many animals and depend on some for our food. A veterinarian or animal doctor is by profession perhaps the greatest humanitarian that one can think of—a very special kind of doctor. We are concerned with both animal life and its effect on human life at the same time. And in treating animal pain and sickness we have to treat dumb creatures since animals can't explain their hurts and feelings like a human can."

This is how Dr. Eugene Adams, a veterinarian, describes his profession. Dr. Adams has been a veterinarian for over 30 years. In the world of animal medicine he has been a meat inspector, teacher, researcher, a designer of veterinary medicine programs in Africa and a pioneer builder of the School of Veterinary Medicine at Tuskegee Institute in Tuskegee, Alabama.

"I had ideas of becoming a dentist when I entered Wichita High School in Wichita, Kansas. But one evening changed all that," said Dr. Adams. "I was attending a father-and-son banquet at the Wichita YMCA. Sitting at a table next to my father and me was a black man, Dr. Thomas G. Perry. He didn't have any children of his own but he was there that evening with another young boy whose father had passed away. Dr. Perry was this boy's father for the evening, and this really impressed me and drew my attention to him.

"As I sat there eating and listening to the various speakers, I began to think about what Dr. Perry did to make a living. He was a veterinarian and the owner of one of the first animal hospitals in Wichita and the entire mid-West in the 1920's."

When the banquet was over young Adams met Dr. Perry briefly. "Could I visit your animal hospital," he asked. "Of course," replied Dr. Perry, little imagining that Gene Adams would follow him into the field of animal medicine.

There was another black man working in public health in Wichita. He was a meat inspector at a local meat packing plant. He prepared slaughtered animals for inspection by veterinarians at the plant. "Between my junior and senior year in high school I needed to earn some money and was able to land a job at the meat plant. And so I learned that caring for dogs and cats wasn't the only kind of work for a veterinarian."

During his senior year, Adams spent time at Dr. Perry's animal hospital. Perry had graduated from the School of Veterinary Medicine at Kansas State University in 1926. He had become one of the first veterinarians to have a successful small animal practice in this country. He was a specialist in the treatment of greyhound racing dogs. His work in the field of veterinary medicine for small animals was widely known in the mid-West during the almost three decades of his practice.

Because of his respect for Dr. Perry, Gene Adams decided on a career in veterinary medicine instead of dentistry. He went to Kansas State University after high school, and after two years of college study, he was ready to apply for admission to School of Veterinary Medicine.

Dr. Perry feared that Adams wouldn't be accepted because he was black, but Gene Adams had studied hard in high school and college. His grades were good, and he was accepted without difficulty. In 1944 he graduated with his doctor's degree in veterinary medicine.

In 1944, World War II was raging on the battlefields of Europe. Dr. Adams wanted to return to Wichita to work with Dr. Perry, but he was eligible to be drafted into the army. His draft board warned him that working at a small animal medical practice in Wichita wasn't essential to the war effort.

White graduates of veterinary schools were being drafted into the army as First Lieutenants. The situation was different for graduates who were black. When Dr. Adams and another black veterinarian arrived at Fort Riley Army Base, they were told that they would have to enter as privates. Adams refused to accept such discriminatory treatment. Instead he decided to work for the United States Government as a civilian.

He was assigned to the Meat Inspection Service of the Department of Agriculture in St. Louis, Missouri. Being a meat inspector was considered essential to the country's war effort.

Meat inspectors examine animal organs for traces of disease. Meat from diseased animals can be dangerous to humans when eaten. From 7,000–8,000 hogs, 400–500 cattle and 300–400 sheep were killed each day, and every animal had to be examined. Dr. Adams had only three assistants, "So I saw a lot of animals," he said.

Dr. Adams remained in St. Louis for seven years, until the war was over and he was no longer eligible to be drafted into the army. But staying out of the army was not the only reason he stayed in St. Louis so long.

After two years as a meat inspector, he felt that he was qualified to become a supervisor at the slaughter house. "Gene, you're as big as you're going to get here," replied the inspector in charge when Dr. Adams asked about a promotion. "What are the qualifications for becoming a supervisor," Adams wanted to know. "Well one of them is to be white," was the reply. Dr. Adams decided to move.

In 1947 there was an outbreak of hoof and mouth disease in Mexico. It was so severe that American vets were being sent to Mexico in large numbers, and Adams thought it would be a good chance for him to leave St. Louis. Again he went to his supervisor. "Well Gene, the only way you could go to Mexico would be for me to declare you surplus—and I'd lose a good man, and I can't do that." That was the last time Dr. Adams went to him for a new assignment.

Dr. Adams' seven years as a meat inspector did furnish one reward. They developed his interest and background in diseases in animals and animal organs, such as the liver, kidneys and brain. He grew to become an outstanding researcher, teacher and leader in the field of animal pathology, the study of the causes and treatment of diseases.

Tuskegee Institute in Alabama is a black college founded by Booker T. Washington in 1881. It was to Tuskegee Institute that George Washington Carver had come in 1896. At Tuskegee his research with the peanut plant revolutionized southern agriculture and improved the health and economy of the country with his peanut products. In 1944 Dr. Perry left Kansas to help start a school of veterinary medicine at Tuskegee, and it was here that Dr. Adams was to find his professional roots.

In 1950 Dr. Adams received an offer to come to Tuskegee to teach. His days as a meat inspector were finally over.

"Coming to Tuskegee was the best decision I have ever made in my life. It gave me the opportunity to advance educationally and to become involved in so many interesting things." During the next 25 years Gene Adams played a major role in building Tuskegee's School of Veterinary Medicine into one of the leading schools of its kind in the country and the world.

From 1951 to 1956 Dr. Adams was an instructor and later an assistant professor in the Department of Pathology and Parasitology at the school. When he arrived at Tuskegee there were few teaching materials in the field of pathology. Not only did he have to prepare animal tissue sections, but in his own words, "I had to learn how to teach pathology to students. I soon realized that to advance as a teacher of animal pathology one has to be on the frontiers of new knowledge through scientific research and further training." So in 1956 Dr. Adams left Tuskegee Institute to attend Cornell University for a year. There he worked and studied as a researcher in pathology and microbiology. In June, 1957, he returned to Tuskegee with a Master of Science degree in comparative pathology and was promoted to the rank of associate professor.

In addition to becoming a skilled medical research scientist at Cornell, Dr. Adams gained new ideas about teaching pathology. "I came back to Tuskegee knowing that pathology must be taught by actually studying disease in real situations, that is, with sick animals brought to a clinic for treatment. We had to begin teaching veterinary students how to relate symptoms of a disease to body organ changes, to blood and

A Tuskeegee Institute student being guided in research in Dr. Adams' laboratory.

urine analysis and tissue examination under a microscope rather than learning about body changes themselves.''

Dr. Adams developed a case history approach to learning about animal disease. He would tell his students that every dead animal has a ''message for us. An animal becomes sick or dies because of a series of things that happened in the animal's body; in pathology the changes in the animal body must be traced carefully to seek and understand the cause of death and illness.''

To further improve his teaching, Dr. Adams returned to

Cornell University in 1959. One of his professors was doing research on leukemia—a type of cancer that affects blood—in cats. This research sparked Dr. Adam's interest in doing research in cancer or tumor pathology.

Cancer is a disease in which some cells in the body begin to produce more and more cells of the same kind in an uncontrolled fashion. The result is a mass of cells, a tumor, that can damage the organs, such as the brain, lungs or bone in which it has grown. One in four people suffer from cancer, and it is the second largest killer of human beings, yet no one knows its exact cause. It can occur in almost any part of the body—the brain, skin, liver, lungs, bone or blood. Often cancer cells spread from one part of the body to another causing damage to healthy, normal body cells and tissues.

The research work of veterinarians like Dr. Adams can lead to important discoveries in the causes and treatment of diseases in humans. Research in animal diseases usually comes before research involving humans. Dr. Adams has devoted over 15 years to studying cancer in dogs and explains the importance of his work this way. "The dog is a good animal model of man. Both are meat eaters, and dogs live close to man, that is, in the same environment. So perhaps what we learn about cancer in dogs may help us to understand cancer in humans."

What is it that causes normal body cells to "run wild" and begin producing more cells or a tumor?

Dr. Adams has studied a tumor in dogs that is transmissible. This means that if cells are taken from a tumor growing in one dog and injected into a healthy dog, the second dog will develop the same kind of tumor. He has discovered that a dog that has survived the growth and surgical removal of a tumor will be immune to new growths. The dog will not grow tumors when injected with the same kind of cancerous cells as before.

Dr. Adams has been able to cultivate or grow the dog tumor cells outside of a dog's body in a test tube, in what is called a tissue culture. He has kept the cells alive in an artificial environment for over eighteen months at a time. This has allowed him to study the cell multiplication activity and is an achievement few researchers have been able to manage.

Dr. Adams has examined the blood from dogs with cancer and has found changes in the amounts of certain proteins in their blood—especially those with tumors caused by cancer cells injected into a healthy dog. The blood protein changes are similar to protein changes caused by virus infections and other infectious diseases in humans and in domestic animals. This may mean that a virus causes tumor growth in dogs.

Dr. Adams' contributions to research and teaching have received national recognition. His cancer research has been commended by both the National Cancer Institute and the U.S. Public Health Service. In 1964 he was the first black person elected to the American College of Veterinary Pathologists. During the same year he received the Norden Award for Distinguished Teaching in the Field of Veterinary Medicine. And when Kansas State University, his alma mater, received a grant from the U.S. government to set up a school of veterinary medicine in Africa, Dr. Adams was asked to head the project.

In June, 1970, Dr. Adams arrived at Ahmadu Bello University at Zaria, North Central Nigeria, Africa. ''When I arrived in Nigeria I saw a chance to repeat some of the same things

I had done at Tuskegee Institute in my earlier years there. Although my job was to develop and teach animal disease and public health courses, there were no teaching materials at hand. The Nigerians also needed applied research. So I could see myself starting out as I had 20 years earlier at Tuskegee.''

Dr. Adams began to develop a program that combined research and teaching. The research had to be related to the problems in Nigeria not those faced in the United States. But all the Nigerian vets had been trained at Tuskegee and knew little about the tropical animal diseases of Africa.

Animals and humans live close together in Africa. Goats, chickens and ducks live in the same quarters as humans. Since tuberculosis is common in cattle, its transfer to humans was a danger in Africa. One of Dr. Adams' first tasks was to document the diseases that were rampant in animals living close to the Nigerians—cattle, horses, poultry, sheep and goats.

Since the Nigerians had no diagnostic program there could be no treatment until Dr. Adams helped to design a diagnostic center where animal blood and feces could be checked for bacteria and parasites. An animal treatment center or clinic was put ''on wheels'' and moved out to the rural areas so people could bring their animals for diagnosis and treatment.

Dr. Adams' training as a meat inspector in St. Louis was helpful in the area of public health. He set up a slaughter house with an inspection program for animals that were to be sold as meat. Parasites which cause sleeping sickness and worms which cause infections were commonly found in the livestock.

Dr. Adams returned to Tuskegee Institute in 1972. He left behind programs to control diseases that could be passed from animals to man, and he had taught improved methods of raising livestock to increase the protein food supply necessary for human health.

The return to Tuskegee marked the beginning of a new important phase of Dr. Adams' work in veterinary medicine. Upon his return he was promoted to Associate Dean of the School of Veterinary Medicine and full professor of veterinary medicine, the positions he now holds.

As associate dean he had new and different responsibilities. He could no longer devote time to teaching. To many students this was a disappointment. One of his former students, Dr. Leon Cruise, wrote to Dr. Adams when he learned that Dr. Adams was not going to be in the classroom:

> . . .Ten years have passed since I graduated from Tuskegee. These years have taught me to appreciate the teaching that you provided to me and those in my class . . . I was somewhat saddened and disappointed to learn that you were no longer available to students as a teacher . . . that you have moved out of the classroom and into an administrative position at the school . . .

Dr. Adams responded to his former student this way:

> . . . My decision to devote most of my time to administration was not an easy one. Perhaps the one event that helped me most to make this decision was a statement made by the head of the Department of Clinical Medicine, School of Veterinary Medicine at Cambridge, England. The essence of his statement was that only those of us who participate actively in both *research* and *teaching* can appreciate the complex problems of moving the total educational program successfully.

> A major concern of mine is to participate in the development of a strong program in teaching and research here in Tuskagee Institute . . .

Tuskegee's School of Veterinary Medicine was established in 1945. At that time there were no schools in the South where students who were black could study veterinary medicine. Dr. Adams had come to Tuskegee in 1950 when the veterinary medicine program was still in its infancy, the first graduates having received their degrees in 1949. Today there are over 500 veterinarians in this country who are black. Nearly 450 graduated from Tuskegee, having studied pathology under Dr. Adams and having received their overall training from a program he spent 25 years helping to build.

Dr. Adams has said that, "Unless more veterinarians can be trained, the nation will be faced with a shortage of more than 10,000 veterinarians by 1980." The educational resources to do the training are the 18 schools of veterinary medicine in the United States. Tuskegee's School of Veterinary Medicine is one of them.

Tuskegee Institute's School of Veterinary Medicine is the only one of the 18 veterinary schools in the United States located at a predominately black college. So, it is in a unique position to help the United States meet its veterinary manpower shortage in a way that no other school can. It can provide the opportunity for black students to enter the health professions through the field of veterinary medicine. Of the nearly 30,000 veterinarians in the United States, less than 600 are black.

The Tuskegee veterinary program has been developed with great difficulty because Tuskegee is a private university and does not receive the same kind of financial support that the other 17 do. They are run by state universities and receive public monies. Tuskegee has served as a national resource in preparing more than 85 percent of the black veterinarians in this country.

Although the school's original purpose was to provide an opportunity for black students in the South to study veterinary medicine, the program, along with others at Tuskegee, is open to all students without regard to race, religion or national background. "We are not operating a black veterinary school but one that happens to be black," says Dr. Adams. The training of vets from outside the United States has always been an important part of Tuskegee's program. Students come from such places as Canada, Haiti, Jamaica, Nigeria, Ethiopia and Puerto Rico. When Dr. Adams arrived in Nigeria in 1970 to teach, he found 16 of his former students working as veterinarians.

Although most veterinarians have private animal hospitals to help sick pets, there are opportunities in a wide variety of jobs in the field of animal medicine. These include working for national, state and city agencies that provide public health services. Over 2,000 veterinarians work for the U.S. Department of Agriculture. Teaching and basic medical research— the roles that Dr. Adams chose—aero-space medicine, radiological health, cattle production and health management, and environmental health and safety are other areas of work for veterinarians. The U.S. Public Health Service, The U.S. Food and Drug Administration and The World Health Organization all employ veterinarians. Many commercial firms use animals and hence veterinary skills in producing and testing medicines, sold in drug stores.

It is people like Dr. Eugene Adams who have made and will continue to make significant contributions to animal and human medicine and health in this country and throughout the world.

ANGELLA D. FERGUSON
1925–
Sickle Cell Researcher, and Hospital Builder

The tiny black baby had just been admitted to the hospital. Her hands and feet were painfully swollen. She lay in her hospital crib, first sobbing then whimpering. Her swollen hands lay stiffly outstretched on the sheets. The child's mother hovered over the bed, helplessly watching her baby's suffering while the doctors tried to find out what was wrong.

The diagnosis was not slow in coming—sickle cell anemia. The baby had inherited the incurable disease from her parents just as she had inherited her brown skin. The mother's sorrow doubled. Not only was her baby very sick, but she and the baby's father had unwittingly given their baby that sickness.

Pain, suffering, sorrowing guilt ridden parents—these are Dr. Angella Ferguson's first memories of a disease which she studied for nearly 20 years of her life. She was a young intern when she recognized that first case of sickle cell anemia. As a medical student, she had learned that sickle cell anemia is a disease that mainly afflicts black people. It was brought to the United States in the blood of African slaves. The disease stems from a defect in the chemical structure of hemoglobin, the oxygen-carrying substance that gives blood its color. Such flawed hemoglobin is called hemoglobin-S. When the body's need for oxygen increases, as in infection or fatigue, hemoglobin-S forms crystallike rods in the blood cells. When this happens, the normally donut-shaped red blood cells are distorted into sicklelike shapes. The misshapen blood cells clog the blood vessels. The result is pain, swelling, and other symptoms brought about by the disruption of the normal flow of life-giving blood.

Persons having sickle cell anemia have inherited the gene for hemoglobin-S from both parents. A person inheriting only one hemoglobin-S gene from one parent is said to have a sickle cell trait. A few of their red blood cells carry hemoglobin-S but seldom do they cause any problems. Such persons may live most of their lives with no knowledge of the trait they carry.

That was what Dr. Angella Ferguson had learned about sickle cell anemia in medical school. She was to add much more to that knowledge.

For Dr. Ferguson, the pediatrics ward was the end of a long career search. The young Washington, D.C., native had started out to be a secretary; then she decided to enter Howard University in Washington, D.C. She chose to study chemistry. Chemistry, she found, was much more interesting than shorthand, but something still seemed to be lacking. "Chemistry is such a dead course," said one of her classmates. She decided to try something living—comparative anatomy. Now she felt she was on the right track. After consulting with her advisor, she signed up for medical school.

As the young medical student donned a white coat and began working in the wards of Freedman's Hospital in Washington, D.C., she found herself increasingly drawn to the sick children and felt a need to help them.

Following her internship, Dr. Ferguson entered a two-year training program in pediatrics. Then she proudly hung out her shingle. But as she began seeing her first patients, she felt the need for more knowledge about black babies. When a mother asked "How soon should my baby crawl? When will she cut a tooth?" Dr. Ferguson was not certain of the answer. She knew that most growth and development norms for children were determined by studying white babies. She wasn't sure at all that such norms fit black babies. She found this lack of knowledge troubling, for only by being certain of the norms can a pediatrician detect the abnormally developing babies. Finally Dr. Ferguson decided to find out for herself what the answers should be to those questions.

She put away her shingle and joined forces with another Washington pediatrician, Dr. Roland Scott. The team launched a study of the growth and development of black babies. Their basic plan was to travel about the country to various hospitals and clinics and study healthy black babies. They used two basic survey techniques—cross sectional and longitudinal. Cross sectional means gathering certain information on all babies of exactly the same age. Longitudinal involves studying a certain child for a certain period of time.

It was in the well-baby clinics that the two researchers made their most significant discovery. These clinics provide health care for newborn babies. Babies are brought in at regular intervals for immunizations and physical exams. Thus Dr. Ferguson was able to follow a healthy child for a year or more. She found that many black babies learned to sit up, pull up and walk faster than many white babies. Why was this? The researchers believed that the answer seemed more related to the environment than to the racial background of the baby. Babies born into poor families did not have playpens or highchairs. They were not restrained from moving about on their own whenever they wished. The children were propped up more and learned to sit sooner. Thus a study that started out to provide better answers about healthy black babies also seemed to provide answers for all healthy babies.

But as Dr. Ferguson studied normal babies, the sight of certain other babies in the clinics and hospitals haunted her.

These were the tiny victims of sickle cell anemia. She began to direct her research activities toward these sufferers.

It was a difficult task she had assigned herself. She knew that the disease was inherited, thus there could be no immediate hope of a cure. The only approach was to study the symptoms and then find ways to relieve those symptoms.

For the sickle cell victim, the worst time is the crisis. Sickle cell crises can strike at any time in any part of the body. The log jam of sickled cells cuts off the flow of blood through blood vessels, triggering such symptoms as pain and swelling due to the damming up of body fluids. Other symptoms, such as skin ulcers and brain damage, may be the result of tissue dying for lack of the nourishing blood. Thus sickle cell crises can mimic heart attack, pneumonia, even brain strokes.

Sorting through the symptoms, Dr. Ferguson and her research team managed to narrow the symptoms down to age groups. They found that from birth to two years, most sickle cell victims suffered arthriticlike symptoms of pain and swelling in the joints, especially the ankles and wrists. Then from age two to six, abdominal pains were the most frequent. These pains were due to the swelling of internal organs, such as the liver and spleen, and caused the child to develop a pot belly. From age six to twelve, the symptoms grew milder. But then at age twelve, the disease flared up again as the child's body began to mature. It was then that the sickle cell victim often developed ulcers on the legs.

But itemizing the symptoms did not always provide a guide for detecting a victim. One tragic case which Dr. Ferguson treated was that of a six-year-old boy who seemed perfectly well until he had his tonsils out. The anesthesia brought on a sickle cell crisis which focused on his brain. He was unconscious and paralyzed for several days. Then slowly he regained consciousness and the use of his body. But over the next 18 months, he had four more brain crises. Finally he died. The autopsy showed a brain almost completely destroyed by the disease. And the boy had had a very high IQ. He had not shown the slightest sign of having sickle cell anemia until his tonsils were removed.

But even out of this tragedy, something was gained. The researchers learned something new about sickle cell anemia. They learned that the sickle cell victim must be given a great deal of oxygen after surgery in order to prevent a crisis.

Once the symptoms had been tracked down, Dr. Ferguson turned her attention to the cause of the crisis.

A kind of diary kept on each small patient provided a day-by-day account of the health happenings in the child's life. Then when a sickle cell crisis developed, Dr. Ferguson simply consulted the diary for clues as to what might have brought on the attack. Quite often the clue was an infection.

Lab tests on the children revealed two other important clues. The blood of the sickle cell victim in crisis was thicker and often more acid than it should be.

Using this information as a guide, Dr. Ferguson set about finding ways to prevent sickle cell crisis. She began by attacking the thick blood problem. Giving fluids through a needle in the vein thinned out the blood. But then she found that simply having the child drink large amounts of water achieved the same effect. She enlisted the parents in the water project. They were advised to keep a jug of water in the refrigerator for the child. Dr. Ferguson would say to the mother, "Tell your child 'Drink that jug empty.' " Since drinking so much water produced another problem, teachers were requested to let the child go to the bathroom as much as possible. Adding small amounts of bicarbonate—an alkaline substance—to the water seemed to adjust the acidity of the blood.

Each patient was put on a program of infection prevention. The children were kept away from people suffering even minor infections. Colds were attacked head on with nosedrops and other medicines. A balanced diet and vitamins built up their resistance. Personal hygiene problems, such as dental work, were taken care of when the child was feeling well.

Out of this beginning grew a kind of guide for treating the child. "We treat the whole child, the student, the family member, as well as the child in crisis," said Dr. Ferguson.

One problem troubling the child in school was the belief of many that sickle cell victims were retarded, unable to learn. A series of tests convinced Dr. Ferguson that such children had normal intelligence. She found that often their appearance only made them seem retarded. Since the bony structure of their heads was affected by the disease, often they had a slight point to their heads. Because their organs were often swollen, they had huge abdomens. They were often very short. Their fingernails and the whites of their eyes were sometimes yellow. But Dr. Ferguson traced most learning problems the children seemed to have to their frequent absenteeism from school due to their health. She recommended tutors and asked teachers to give such children special attention.

Dr. Ferguson also found that the parents of the sickle cell

victim needed attention. They often felt guilty when they found the child had inherited the disease from them. The guilt, the financial strain, the care of a child sick on and off, took their toll on the parents. Sometimes they took out the strain on the child by denying affection. More often, they spoiled the child. And this produced problems among the other children in the family. Sometimes it helped to give the parents psychological counseling. Often just explaining why the parent shouldn't feel guilty for passing on the disease to the child helped. But always the parents were made to understand they were an important part of the health team treating the child.

During the time that Dr. Ferguson was devoting her attention to the symptoms and treating the whole child, other scientists were studying ways to change the shape of the sickled red cell. Many chemicals, such as urea and cyanate compounds, were tried. As Dr. Ferguson learned of these new ideas, she tried them on her patients. Some worked, some did not. But most were dangerous chemicals, too dangerous she felt to give a child for any length of time.

Then, in the late 1960's sickle cell anemia began to get a lot of publicity. Researchers anxious to get funds for research were trying all sorts of treatments for sickle cell. After years of careful study of the disease, Dr. Ferguson knew that some ideas being proposed wouldn't work. For example, some scientists wanted to experiment with exchange blood transfusions in which the patient's blood would be removed and replaced with that of a normal person. Dr. Ferguson knew that the patient's body would replace the normal blood cells with sickled ones. Exchange transfusion was a painful and temporary solution at best.

Some businessmen actually used the disease as an advertising gimmick. Gas stations offered to donate to sickle cell research if people would buy gasoline. Dr. Ferguson was disgusted at the sensationalism now beginning to surround the tragic disease. She felt that future research should be aimed at changing the genes in the sickle cell victims' cells so that their bodies would no longer produce abnormal hemoglobin-S. But before such a thing would be possible, much more must be learned about the gene. Feeling that she had done all she could in sickle cell research, she shut down her research.

For a while it seemed that she would go back to teaching at Howard University Medical School and private practice.

Then, quite unexpectedly, Howard University offered her the chance to do something different. Wouldn't she like to oversee the construction of the new Howard University Hospital? She took the assignment. The hospital stood for something that was sorely needed by the black community of Washington, D.C. For the last 100 years, Freedman Hospital had borne the major burden of the health needs and medical education of Washington's black people. Student doctors and nurses from Howard University crowded into the antiquated structure to be trained in their professions. The hospital was built on the old big ward concept. Thirty patients shared each ward and one bathroom. Then, in the 1960's the federal government decided to build a new hospital for Howard.

As Dr. Ferguson took on her new duties, she found that her major task was convincing those congressmen who controlled the budget for the new hospital that a teaching hospital had to be bigger than a community hospital. She had to point out that more room is needed around a patient's bed so that medical students can learn from physicians treating patients. More consulting rooms would be needed where professors and doctors could talk to students about patients. Research labs and library rooms would be needed. A grand argument was waged over the size of the kitchen area. Dr. Ferguson had to explain that test kitchens would be needed for dietetic interns.

Dr. Ferguson kept the patients in mind, too. She insisted on semi-private rooms and the best decorations—bright colors, carpets throughout, music piped in, even landscaping.

When she was finished she had pushed a $17 million budget to $43 million. But she had produced a modern teaching hospital, more than twice as large as Freedman's and equipped with the most up-to-date medical facilities.

Finally, as the glass and stone building took shape and moving day approached, Dr. Ferguson found she had one more major battle to fight. Neighborhood children found that the expensive parking lot lights made great targets. One night, just before Thanksgiving, they broke 30 of the $110 lights.

Dr. Ferguson decided that the children needed to understand that the hospital was theirs. They were taken on a tour of the new building and then given Thanksgiving dinner. They were organized into the Courtesy Patrol and given orange jackets to wear. They began to serve the hospital by conducting tours, filling in on elevators and at the reception desk. And no more lights were broken. "Orange jackets" were not even seen walking on the grass.

For Dr. Ferguson the future seemed bright. There was a new cancer wing going up soon and plans to add on to the medical school and the dental school . . . and a new convalescent care building was in the works . . .

INDEX

ACKNOWLEDGEMENTS

Photographs and quotation are reproduced courtesy of the following:

pages 14, 24   Solomon C. Fuller, Jr.
page 30   Mrs. Gertrude Donaghue
page 38   *Ebony Magazine*, Johnson Publications
page 46   Mrs. Louis T. Wright
page 64   W. Montague Cobb
page 71   National Medical Association
page 78   New York Times/Tyrone Dukes
page 90   Daniel Collins
page 94   Quotation reprinted by permission from *The Interpreter*, Jan. 1972, published by Joint Committee on Communications of the United Methodist Church.
page 108   Jane Wright
pages 118, 125   Eugene Adams
page 132   Angella Ferguson

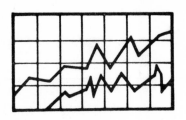

THIS BOOK BELONGS TO:

_____

_____

_____